BUDDHIST WISDOM FOR BEGINNERS

A GUIDE FROM A TO Z

Sunstone books may be purchased for educational, business, or sales promotional use.
For information please write: Special Markets Department, Sunstone Press,
P.O. Box 2321, Santa Fe, New Mexico 87504-2321.
Printed on acid-free paper
∞
eBook 978-1-61139-695-9

———————————

Library of Congress Cataloging-in-Publication Data

Names: Parachin, Victor M., author.
Title: Buddhist wisdom for beginners : a guide from A to Z / Victor M.
    Parachin, M. Div.
Description: Santa Fe : Sunstone Press, [2023] | Summary: "A basic
    introduction to the philosophies and practices of Buddhism as well as
    ways to incorporate them into daily life"-- Provided by publisher.
Identifiers: LCCN 2023018427 | ISBN 9781632935298 (paperback) | ISBN
    9781611396959 (epub)
Subjects: LCSH: Buddhism. | Buddhist philosophy.
Classification: LCC BQ4022 .P37 2023 | DDC 294.3--dc23/eng/20230426
LC record available at https://lccn.loc.gov/2023018427

———————————

WWW.SUNSTONEPRESS.COM
SUNSTONE PRESS / POST OFFICE BOX 2321 / SANTA FE, NM 87504-2321 /USA
(505) 988-4418

BUDDHIST WISDOM FOR BEGINNERS

A Guide from A to Z

Victor M. Parachin, M. Div.

SUNSTONE
PRESS

SANTA FE

INTRODUCTION

We have to live wisely; incline our lives toward truth;
continuously undercut and diminish selfishness; and
develop poise, alertness, and kindness so that the real,
loving, compassionate being who we are can be here
in this present moment, where enlightenment can happen.
                                                    —Ajahn Sumano

Buddhism is primarily a wisdom tradition.

With wisdom, we act skillfully and compassionately. Our lives operate at optimal levels generating feelings of happiness and contentment, peace and harmony.

Without wisdom we are reactive and impulsive, blundering along. Our lives become deeply dysfunctional and highly defective.

It is the wisdom path first taught by the Buddha, and later by his followers over thousands of years, shows us how to evolve and expand spiritually, mentally, emotionally and socially.

This A-Z Guide of Buddhist wisdom for beginners offers information, insight and inspiration for living with greater awareness and opens the door to an enlightened life.

A

ACCOUNTABILITY

A LESSON FROM A CARPET MERCHANT

Promises are only as strong as the person who gives them.
—Stephen Richards

A merchant who, after spending time in retreat at a Buddhist monastery, promised the abbot he would give the center a beautiful carpet. However, the carpet was never delivered so, after some time, the abbot send a disciple to ask the merchant about it. The merchant said "Oh, thank you for reminding me. I'd forgotten about it. I shall give the monastery a carpet twice a large and twice as thick." He retrieved the carpet from his inventory giving it to the disciple who was angry because now he had a very heavy load to carry all the way back to the monastery.

As he lugged the carpet back with some local help, he kept thinking to himself: "This is all very odd. The abbot constantly reminds us to live simply and be unattached to things. Yet, here I am bringing back a carpet that he wants."

When he arrived back at the monastery, he threw the carpet onto the ground and said loudly to the abbot: "Here's your carpet!"

Sensing his anger, the abbot asked: "What's going on with you?"

"Well, you keep teaching us to live simply and remain unattached to things yet you had me go all the way to the market to bring back this carpet."

The abbot explained: "The merchant voluntarily promised to give a carpet to the monastery. Would you rather see him be on the receiving end of some very bad karma for breaking his word?"

This simple story is about accountability. When we tell someone we will do something, we must feel a responsibility to follow through and keep our word. If we do not, there is an immediate karmic result, that of a space being created between ourself and the person to whom we made a promise. If the pattern continues whereby we commit to doing something for the person and then not doing it, then the distance will expand. Eventually that person will come to view us as unreliable and untrustworthy. Sometimes the distance created when promises aren't kept become so large they cannot be bridged.

ANGER

TREATMENT FOR ANGER

Anger doesn't just happen to us. If we're able to
catch an angry thought as it's budding, we can let it go.
　　　　　　　　　　　　　　　—John Daido Loori

With permission from the monastery Abbott, a monk borrowed an old boat and rowed out into the middle of a lake for his afternoon meditation session. It was a truly peaceful place to meditate as the boat gently floated.

After more than an hour of undisturbed silence, he felt the bump of another boat bang against his. With eyes still closed, he could feel anger swelling within himself at the careless boatman who didn't prevent the lake collision.

Upon opening his eyes, all he saw was an empty boat which he realized had obviously become untied from the dock and merely drifted out into the lake bumping up against his. Immediately, the monk experienced a flash of enlightenment, one which would serve him well for the rest of his life. "The anger is within me," he thought to himself. "All anger needs is a bump from the outside to be triggered and provoked out of me."

From that moment on, whenever another person irritated him and he could feel even the slightest anger rising, he gently reminded himself: "The other person is an empty, floating boat. The anger is within me."

ANIMALS

THE GOLDEN RULE APPLIED TO ANIMALS

Whether they be creatures of the land or air, whoever harms
here any living being, who has no compassion for all that live,
let such a one be known as depraved.
　　　　　　　　　　　　　　　—Buddha

What's called the 'golden rule'—*do to others what you would want them to do for you*—is found in all religious traditions including Buddhism. However, the Buddha expanded the golden rule applying it to our treatment of animals who share the planet with us.

Modern Chinese Buddhist teacher Hsing Yun tells about a time when he was seven years of age and boy came across a group of chicks caught in a bitterly cold Chinese winter rain. Feeling sorry for them because of their soaked condition he took them into his one room family home and tried to dry their feathers in front of the stove. The chicks, not understanding what was happening panicked with one accidentally jumping into the stove. By the time he was able to pull it back out of the fire, all it's feathers had been badly burned and it's little feet scorched from the coals. It's lower beak had been broken.

Every day after that, Hsing Yun patiently hand fed that injured little chick, one mouthful at a time. As he fed it, he spoke to it in a soft, loving, tone. He did that for an entire year before the chick fully regained its health. A few months after that, it became a very strong hen and was able to lay eggs with the rest of her companions.

Hsing Yun says that his family and neighbors were surprised at his patience and achievement in nursing a little chick back to health. They asked him how he did that and what was the technique. His answer reflects the golden rule: "I imagined I was that tiny chick. With that state of mind, I gave what I thought the chick needed most."

ASSOCIATIONS

RIGHT ASSOCIATION

If you find no one to support you on the spiritual path, walk alone. If you see a wise person who steers you away from the wrong path, follow him. The company of the wise is joyful, like reunion with one's family. Therefore, live among the wise, who are understanding, patient, responsible and noble.

—The Dhammapada

One of the earliest summaries of the Buddha's teachings are contained in the Noble Eightfold Path—right view, right attitude, right speech, right action, right livelihood, right effort, right mindfulness. Though those eight steps on the path are comprehensive, this ninth step could naturally be added: right association.

Having right associations was clearly and consistently emphasized by the Buddha, so much so that it is appropriate to consider it as a ninth step on the path. The truth is that we are greatly influenced, positively and negatively, the people we associate with the most. Here are three key ways to create right associations.

First, surround yourself with positive, optimistic, joyful people. Little by little, reduce and eventually, remove from your close circle people who are negative, cynical and prone to drama.

Secondly, be part of a spiritual community such as a yoga class, meditation group, or a among people who meet regularly to study religious texts. In Buddhism such a group is called the sangha or association while among Hindus it's referred to as satsang or the community of truth.

Thirdly, read or listen to teachings which are informative and inspiring. Though we cannot always be in the presence of gifted teachers, we can still benefit from them by reading their writings and listening or viewing their talks.

So important are right associations that the Buddha said "if you find no one to support you on the spiritual path, walk alone."

AUTHENTIC

AUTHENTIC GENEROSITY

*When you are practicing generosity, you should feel a
little pinch when you give something away. That pinch
is your stinginess protesting.*

—Gelek Rinpoche

A martial arts teacher recalls a time when one of her young students came to class without his purple belt. She promptly reminded him it was part of his discipline and responsibility to have his uniform and belt with him at class at all times.

"Where is your belt," she asked.

The boy looked downward embarrassed saying he didn't have it.

"Do you know where it is?" she repeated.

"My baby sister died, and I put it in her coffin to take to heaven with her," the boy responded.

Immediately his instructor understood the depth of his action as tears welled in her eyes. Later she shared that incident with her own instructor saying: "That belt was probably his most important possession."

Clearly this young man knew the meaning of authentic generosity and knew how to give away his best.

AWAKENING

YOU MAY BE AN AWAKENED PERSON IF...

*The pursuit of enlightenment is for the purpose of the
world, not merely for the purpose of the individual.
Practices for enlightenment must lead to action in
the world.*

—Bernie Glassman

Evidence of our spiritual awakening is present in the way we live out our day to day lives. In a humorous way, Ram Dass said: "If you think you are enlightened, go home for Thanksgiving." We are awakened (enlightened) women and men if...

We are less preoccupied with ourselves and more concerned about helping others;

We naturally, spontaneously express kindness, compassion, acceptance, love;

We are patient with others and with ourselves;

We are generally peaceful and serene;

We are generous with our time, talent and material possessions;

We feel both sadness and compassion for the condition of the world;

We wish to relieve suffering of other beings;

We realize that life is precious to all, human and all sentient beings— animals, fish, insects.

We enjoy nature and being outside—it's not a coincidence the Buddha became enlightened while meditating outside, under a tree.

B

BALANCE

REMAINING BALANCED

*One needs physical, mental and inner spiritual strength
at all times. One requires this inner strength especially
during the time of disturbance, agitation and confusion.*
—Swami Sivananda

During a civil war in Japan, militias often invaded little villages. In one village everyone heard solders were coming and fled. When the militia arrived the village was vacant...except for one person, a zen master who remained to take care of the temple. The general of the army went to the temple to see who this lone inhabitant.

When he arrived the master didn't bow or grovel. He didn't even speak to the general at all. Feeling disrespected, the general became angry. He drew his sword and shouted, "You fool. Don't you realize I could run you through without blinking an eye?" The Zen calmly replied, "Do you realize I could be run through without blinking an eye?" Surprised and awed by the master, the general simply left.

This encounter, which is a popular teaching in the Zen tradition, is about equanimity or balance in the presence of various life issues. Using the prospect of one's death, which is for many the greatest life fear, the story teaches that one can face anything—including death—in a balanced way. There is no need to react, cringe in fear, or panic.

Equanimity is something which ought to be brought into all events which come our way. In times of pain and pleasure, in times of sorrow and happiness, we can train ourselves not be carried away by our emotions remembering to remain in a balanced state.

For example, when we learn someone has gossiped about us we do not react by gossiping back nor feeling broken by what was said. When we are treated with contempt and rudeness, we do not lash out with anger. Or, when someone we love has been diagnosed with a life threatening illness, we do not collapse in dread. We choose to remain balanced, calm, even serene.

BETTER

BECOME A BIGGER, BETTER VERSION OF YOURSELF

Even if you fail a thousand times, be steadfast.
Eventually you will succeed in uplifting your personality.
—Swami Jyotirmayananda

Accessing your Buddha Nature or Christ Consciousness or Inner Divinity or your Higher Self is not as complicated and difficult as some make it out to be.

Here are five steps for becoming a better, bigger, higher version of yourself:

1. Identify three qualities or virtues which you'd like develop. Choose ones which you already admire in other people. For example people who are encouraging, kind, peaceful.

2. Begin to express those three in all your daily activities—working, speaking, acting, thinking.

3. Each evening before drifting off to sleep, review the day racking where you've been successful; where more effort is required.

4. If you see an area of weakness, don't justify it or excuse it. Also, don't become overly disappointed and frustrated with yourself. Doing so will simply suffocate your commitment.

5. Start again in the morning. "Even if you fail a thousand times, be steadfast, Eventually you will succeed in uplifting your personality."

—Notes of Swami Jyotirmayananda

BIRTHDAYS

MINDFUL BIRTHDAYS

One should not remember one's day of birth with
a hedonistic celebration.

—Sheng Yen

The quote above from contemporary Zen master Sheng Yen is not a rejection of a birthday celebration. The word 'hedonistic' simply means 'self-indulgent'. The Buddhist view and the one promoted by Sheng Yen, is to celebrate one's birthday _and_ expand that festive occasion to embrace others. Here are three specifically Buddhist (mindful) ways to celebrate a birthday.

First, remember, with appreciation, the woman who gave you birth. Whether your mother was adequate or not is irrelevant. The fact is, she kept you alive and nurtured your growth when you could not do it yourself. For that, the woman who birthed you should be a focus of gratitude.

Secondly, do an act of kindness for an animal. On special days, Buddhists worldwide will go to a market and buy a live creature destined for slaughter—a fish, goat, sheep, turtle, bird—and release it in an appropriate area. As this custom may be less viable in urban settings, another way to embrace animal compassion on a birthday is by making significant donation to an animal shelter.

Thirdly, create a more mindful birthday by contributing a gift of money to a needy individual (a student, single parent, struggling senior citizen) or to a civic organization.

By so doing, a birthday isn't just "all about me" but is also about others.

BLOOM

BLOOM WHERE YOU ARE PLANTED

One must allow the springs, summers, autumns, and winters,
the winds, frosts, rains and snows to become
causes and conditions of one's growth.

—Hsing Yun

This popular aphorism is a reminder to make the best of whatever situation we find ourselves. It is especially applies to the tough experiences which come our way, unwelcome and uninvited. Here are ten ways to bloom where you are planted:

1. Learn to shine your light when a great darkness has come upon you.
2. Chose hope over despair, optimism over pessimism.
3. Don't complain. It extinguishes whatever joys struggle to emerge.
4. Change. If your circumstance can't be changed, then change your attitude.
5. Help others. Take the focus off yourself, your problem and help another person.
6. Identify positives. Perhaps you're learning resilience; perhaps you're discovering who your real friends are; perhaps you're tapping into strengths you were not aware of.
7. Grow through the cracks. A beautiful flower can emerge from a small sidewalk crack. Do the same. If your family is dysfunctional, grow through whatever 'cracks' are available. If your work environment is toxic, find the 'cracks' and grow. Your growth can take place in spite of what surrounds you.
8. Make sure you are watered. Without the nourishment of water, plants will dry up and die. Be sure you engage in self-care, especially while doing through a hard time.
9. Get plenty of sunshine. To bloom every flower needs the warmth of the sun. Surround yourself with individuals who bring you light. Read material which not only informs but inspires you.
10. Be patient. Flowers don't bloom over night.

BREATH

BREATHE BETTER TO FEEL BETTER

Breath is the link between the mental and physical disciplines. It makes the mind calm, lucid and steady.
—Swami Vishnu Devananda

Most of us take the breath for granted until breath becomes a struggle as when walking up a flight of stairs huffing, puffing and gasping for breath. Or, during a time of great anxiety when suddenly breathing becomes erratic and we feel as if we're suffocating.

Not only do most people take breath for granted but many people do not breathe properly. Consistent ineffective breathing eventually results in fatigue, stress, anxiety, illness and a wide variety of other health issues.

To determine if you are a good breather or a weak breather, take a few moments and pay attention to your breath. As you inhale and exhale sense whether your breathing is shallow and rapid or smooth and steady? Because both body and mind are affected—negatively or positively—by the way we breath it's important to so properly.

Here is a simple but powerful yoga way to improve breathing. It's done in three phases:

1. Inhalation. (Inhale slowly and smoothly)
2. Retention. (Hold the breath for just a few seconds not to the point of stress)
3. Exhalation. (Intentionally make the exhalation much longer than the inhalation)

Initially repeat for five minutes gradually working your way up to 10 or 15 minutes of this breath exercise.

BUDDHA NATURE

TAPPING INTO YOUR BUDDHA NATURE

We are, by nature, endowed with qualities of absolute goodness—purest love, compassion, wisdom and tranquility.

—John Makransky

Buddhism teaches that all beings have Buddha nature, meaning, they have innate wisdom, goodness, compassion and more.

Consider the outlaw Jesse James who, for a moment, tapped into his Buddha nature. While on the run and in hiding from the law, James and his gang sought food and rest at a remote farmhouse. The woman who lived there greeted the men warmly, responding to their request for food and a time to rest safely. As she prepared the meal for them, she apologized for her meager resources explaining she was recently widowed, had no income and was unable to keep up with the farm mortgage. In fact, a banker was on his way to foreclose on her farm unless she could give him the $1,400 she owed.

James had with him a sack full of money from one of his raids. He gave the astonished woman $1,400 she needed to pay off the debt instructing her, "Be sure you get a receipt when you pay the banker." As James and his gang prepared to leave, he reminded the widow once again, "Be sure to get a receipt when you pay the banker."

A short time later, the banker arrived at the widow's farm looking grim and unhappy to be foreclosing on her. When he emerged from the house, the banker looked relieved because the woman was able to pay off the debt. As he rode off the property, Jesse James and the gang stopped him, recovered their $1,400 and rode off.

Don't let some flaws and failures prevent you from tapping into and acting on your innate Buddha nature.

C

COMMITMENT

ASSESS YOUR COMMITMENTS

Everything you do is right, nothing you do is wrong;
yet you must still make ceaseless effort.
—Shunryu Suzuki

One day, while staying at a friend's house, Nasrudin peered over the wall into the neighbor's yard where he was mesmerized by the most beautiful garden he had ever seen. It was immaculate with magnificent flowers blooming. He noticed an old man patiently weeding a flower-bed and asked: "This is a beautiful garden. I'd like to have one just like it. How do you make a garden like this? What is the technique?" The gardener replied: "Twenty years, hard work" to which Nasrudin responded: "Never mind."

Nasrudin was a 13th century Sufi mystic well known and well liked for his use of satire and humor to teach spiritual lessons. This story is about commitments and making an assessment of their depth and importance in your life.

For example, you may want to have a strong meditation practice perhaps one like someone you know and admire. You begin and move ahead with the greatest of intentions but then the practice begins to dwindle away due to a variety of reasons—discouragement at not seeing the desire results, the pressures of time, or boredom. You know meditation is a good thing so why don't you keep doing it?

Nasrudin's story casts a wide net applying itself to other situations such as quitting smoking, exercising regularly, dieting, stop gossiping, be a more positive person, maintaining a good relationship with someone, etc. The lesson he's conveying is a simple one: commitments require labor. An true and honest commitment means doing it day after day and doing so even when the going is tough. To have a beautiful "garden" of any kind can take "twenty years, hard work."

COMPASSION

EQUAL COMPASSION

We must reduce our own negativity and learn to develop equal love and compassion for all beings. Equal compassion is truly great compassion.

—Chagdud Tulku

On January 20, 1948, exactly ten days before he was assassinated, a handmade bomb was hurled at Mahatma Gandhi as he participated in a gathering made up primarily of people from the Sikh religion. It was an act of terrorism carried out by a young person unhappy with Gandhi's philosophy. Gandhi survived and the youth was immediately captured.

The next day several Sikhs called on Gandhi expressing support and assurance that the bomber was not a Sikh. Gandhi responded gently saying it didn't matter to him whether the assailant was a Sikh, Hindu or Muslim. In fact, he added, whoever the attempted assassin was he only wished him well explaining that the young man was a victim; that he had been taught to think of Gandhi as an enemy of the Hindu cause; that hatred had been transplanted into his heart by others. The youth had been persuaded to think that things in India were so desperate that the only solution was violence.

Gandhi said he felt only compassion for the youth and no anger. Additionally, Gandhi asked the embarrassed and outraged chief of police not to mistreat the youth but to make every effort to help him right his thoughts and actions.

Some people felt Gandhi was naive in this approach saying his attitude was unrealistic, sentimental and dangerous. Gandhi was unmoved and continued to practice equal compassion for all.

CONSEQUENCES

THE CHAIN OF MONKEYS

Sometimes when I consider what tremendous consequences come from little things ... I am tempted to think there are no little things.

—Bruce Barton

The king of the monkeys was wandering through a forest one evening when he came to the edge of a cliff. Looking down far below he saw the bright moon reflected on the river waters. "That is a magnificent jewel," he said to himself adding "and I must have it."

He brought his desire to other monkeys, all of whom objected saying it would be nearly impossible to get down that far from the cliff and retrieve the jewel. The monkey king overruled them saying: "I have a plan. One monkey can hold onto a tree and all other monkeys will form a line with each one holding tightly to the tail of the monkey in front. Then we can lower our monkey chain down to the water and the last monkey will be able to reach the jewel retrieving it for me." The group thought it could be done so 500 monkeys dangled down to the water but the weight was too much for the one holding the tree and all five hundred monkeys fell into the water and drowned.

That popular Eastern story is a lesson about the mind. Too often we have "monkey minds" which do not consider carefully enough the consequences of an action before it is taken. While we are free to choose our actions, we are not free to choose the consequences of those actions. That is the law of Karma which operates through the universe. People have experienced tremendous sadness because of careless thinking and acting saying "I didn't mean for it to turn out like this."

The way to avoid such troubles and tragedies lies in mind management. It is important to think things through, consider all options, and take the most skillful action. Only then are the odds in our favor that the consequences will be positive rather than negative and disappointing.

CRAVING

HOW MUCH DO YOU REALLY NEED?

Simple living helps in high thinking and getting mastery over mind and body.
                                        —Swami Sivananda

The Buddha recognized that we humans have four basic needs. In Buddhism these are referred to as "The Four Requisites" which are:

1. Nutrition—food and water to keep the body healthy and strong.

2. Clothing—to protect from the elements and from insects.

3. Shelter—for safety and protection from weather conditions.

4. Medicine—to help the body overcome disease.

These are basic and necessary. However, this list of four then raise these important questions:

1. How much food do you really need?

2. How much clothing do you really need?

3. How much shelter do you really need?

4. How much medicine do you really need?

So much of what we "need" is driven by advertising and resulting consumerism. This constant pressure produces craving and the results aren't healthy:

1. Obesity.

2. Closets bulging with clothes and shoes seldom worn.

3. Huge houses often referred to as "McMansions."

5. Health care costs soaring.

Can you incorporate these concepts, words and phrases into your life: *cutting back, scaling down, reducing, donating, trimming, winding back, phase out, shrink?*

D

DEEPEN

DEEPEN YOUR MEDITATION PRACTICE.

Meditation is a great gift to give yourself. It is a way to experience a higher quality of life just by going inside yourself and touching your center for a moment. It is a brief retreat from the world that lets you reenter the world with a more vivid presence .
—Lorin Roche

1. Do it with a group. Worldwide, Buddhist monks spend most of their time in group meditation. The reason for that is simple: it's the easiest way to do meditation. The energy of several people sitting together is motivating and makes it possible to sit longer. Most group meditation sessions are at least one hour.

2. Do it with a friend. This way you both support and encourage each other to deepen the practice.

3. Do it alone. Tap your inner Buddha and find a quiet place to sit. Do it several times a week. Daily if possible.

4. Do it with a teacher. One of the best ways to begin mediation or deepen a practice is to take some private instruction from a meditation teacher.

5. Do it outside. Be like the ancient yogis who did a lot of their meditation outside. Nature nurtures the spirit and stimulates the senses. There are flowers to see, grasses to smell, birds to hear. All of those can create a sense of peace, awe and unity with the planet.

6. Do it with children. Introduce meditation a child: yours, a niece, a nephew, a godchild, etc. Children are naturals for this practice when given user friendly instructions. In doing this you will provide them with a powerful tool they can tap into in the years ahead.

7. Do it at work. Instead of taking that coffee break and adding caffeine to work stress, use the break time to meditate in your office or cubicle. Consider also sitting quietly over lunch.

8. Do it with a student. Offer to teach someone to mediate. Find someone interested and make the suggestion. Many people want to learn meditation but don't know how to get started. Open that door for them.

9. Do it at a temple. I often meditate at a Hindu Temple in my city. It's open every morning and every evening for several hours. Visitors are always welcome to come inside and simply sit.

10. Just do it! Keep it short or keep it long or somewhere in between. Just do it! Remember than a few minutes of meditation is better than no meditation at all.

DIFFICULT

DEALING WITH DIFFICULT PEOPLE

Human decency should not depend on our ability to muster a feeling of love for the other.
　　　　　　　　　　　　　　　　　　—Rabbi Arthur Green

What is the correct way to deal with some human beings who are especially obnoxious, unkind and unlovable because of their actions? As citizens of the planet are we obliged to love them?

That question is frequently dealt with in Judaism and Jewish teaching offers this positive insight. If we encounter people who act in unfriendly, hostile ways toward us, love is not a basic rule of the Jewish Torah.

However, we are to remember that they are created in the image of God and must be treated that way even if we cannot love them. That's why Rabbi Arthur Green says "human decency should not depend on our ability to muster a feeling of love for the other."

This Jewish teaching translated well into Buddhist thinking. Every person—regardless how disgraceful and disgusting his or her behavior may be—has Buddha nature, has the potential to emerge into full Buddhahood. While we may not need to love them, we must work to see and respect their inner Buddha nature. And, when possible, do what we can to support its growth. Every human being, through practice and with some assistance from others, can become an enlightened one.

HOW BUDDHA DEALT WITH DIFFICULT PEOPLE

The one characteristic of authentic power that most people overlook is humbleness. It is important for many reasons. A humble person walks in a friendly world.
—Gary Zukav

Far too often we encounter difficult people, those who are inconsiderate, rude, arrogant, ignorant and even unkind. These types of individuals have always been around and even in his day, the Buddha had to deal with them. Actually, the Buddha taught that we should be grateful for difficult people because they helped us refine and develop good character.

Based upon his own interactions, the Buddha instructed his followers to practice discipline and patience in four unpleasant situations.

First, when others become angry with you, do not react with anger but with discipline and patience. Secondly, if another person strikes you, do not retaliate or return blows. Thirdly, when others criticize you, do not criticize them in retaliation. Fourthly, when others insult you, do not respond by insulting or embarrassing them.

Anticipating that followers might find these instructions challenging and even unrealistic, the Buddha explained there were these four corresponding advantages—followers will improve their patience and discipline, bring harmony to their relationships, create more social goodwill and move more rapidly to awakening.

DISAPPROVAL

SOMETIMES YOU HAVE TO HISS

*There are moments when a critical sensibility
in life is appropriate.*

—Victor M. Parachin

There is a fascinating Buddhist tale about a cobra who encountered a meditation master and asked how to meditate and become enlightened. The cobra was instructed to practice loving kindness toward all beings and was taught to recite this loving kindness mantra:

May all beings be healthy;
May all beings be happy;
May all beings be safe;
May all beings be free of suffering.

Faithfully, the cobra recited the mantra and put loving kindness into action. Early one morning a woman was in the forest collecting fallen branches and pieces of wood to use for a fire. Mistaking the cobra for a piece of rope she picked it up and used the cobra to tie a bundle of wood. Though this caused pain to the cobra, it remained silent. When the cobra managed to escape later, the creature had scratches and cuts all over its body.

Meeting with the meditation master, the cobra lamented: "Look what has happened to me. I adopt the practice of loving-kindness and all it's done is brought me pain and wounds!" Very kindly and gently, the master responded: "In that case you were not practicing loving kindness. You were engaged in the practice of foolish loving kindness. By simply hissing, you could have shown the woman you were a cobra."

Here's the lesson: sometimes you have to hiss; sometimes you have to express disapproval; sometimes it's appropriate to convey dissatisfaction.

DISCRIMINATION

PUTTING AN END TO DISCRIMINATION

The only way to change bad habits, prejudicial life patterns and negative behaviors is to first change our thinking.
> —Victor M. Parachin

Prior to becoming the fifth director of the Federal Bureau of Investigation, Louis. J. Freeh was a Federal Judge and recalls being assigned a court case which affected him in a deeply personal way. He was randomly assigned a case involving a woman alleging sexual discrimination against the Wall Street firm she worked at.

Freeh looked at the firm's name and immediately his memory took him back thirty years earlier to a story his mother told him. She had just completed high school and was seeking her first job in New York City. Learning about an opening at a Wall Street firm she went and filled out an application. A friend who worked there told her she would be a good fit with the company. A subsequent interview went very well. Though there were three other applicants, Freeh's mother appeared to be at the top of the list. She was called for an additional interview and, finally after waiting most of an afternoon, the personnel director came and told Freeh's mother: "We'd like to employ you but we don't hire Italians."

So, it turned out that thirty years the woman's son—Louis Freeh— was assigned a case which clearly revealed that the same company was continuing to operate in the same discriminatory way but now substituting gender for country of origin. Of course, Freeh recused himself from presiding over the case.

That incident raises these intriguing questions. How is it that company leaders, year after year, continue to follow a pattern which is unfair and unjust? How is it that the managers of that firm—all likely highly educated—could continue to perpetuate a leadership style so inequitable?

The issue is one of thinking and their inability or unwillingness to challenge and change their thoughts. That's why it is important that we are always vigilant about what we think because actions follow thoughts. The only way to change life patterns and behaviors is to first change our thinking. No one has to remain a bigot. Transformation is always possible.

E

EFFORT

RIGHT EFFORT

Cultivate thoughts and actions which support,
not erode, an enlightened mind.

—Victor M. Parachin

To evolve morally and spiritually, Buddhism offers the eightfold noble path. Number
six is "right effort", the cultivating of positive qualities and releasing negative ones. Buddhism fine tunes right effort into sub categories called "four big efforts."

1. The effort to avoid negative not yet existing in our lives.
2. The effort to overcome negative which already exists in our thoughts and acts.
3. The effort to preserve the positive already developed in our thinking and acting.
4. The effort to develop the positive not yet existing in our minds, hearts and actions.

Driving the four big efforts teaching is the understanding that too many people have right intentions but neglect to put good ideas into practice, into daily life. This weakness is further strengthened by putting off for another day what we know should be done today. That's why it's important to cultivate the four great efforts daily—to avoid, overcome, preserve, and develop.

ENERGY

WHY YOUR ENERGY IS LOW

*You will have to abandon an old idea, however strong
and ingrained it may be, when you get a new elevating
idea in its stead.*

—Swami Sivananda

Each one of us experiences times when our energies are on low. Often it's just a passing phase, but sometimes low energy persists for weeks or months at a time. Excluding some physical issue, which could be addressed by a medical professional, there can be other reasons why you are losing energy. Consider these:

The company you keep. Some individuals are energy "vampires." They literally suck the life out of you.

Poor breathing. The most relaxed and motivating breathing is when we take long inhales and exhales. Rapid, shallow breathing is draining.

Unhealthy diet. Too much restaurant food; too much processed food,; too few fresh fruits, vegetables and whole grains.

Lack of exercise. Inactivity and being glued to a screen of some kind isn't good for body, mind or spirit.

Wrong lifestyle. Being a 'party animal', consuming copious amounts of alcohol, and other forms of self indulgence deplete vitality.

Stress and anxiety. A mind infected with worries can't relax. Set some time aside for meditation to clear the mind and calm the spirit.

Employment. So many workplaces are toxic for a variety of reasons. While you may not be able to quit your job immediately, it's worth making an assessment with a view to soon changing it.

Your family. We have no choice about our family of origin but when a family is highly dysfunctional and draining you, it's time to choose to create a new "family" made up of people who lift you up, inspire and motivate you..

Take an inventory of your life to establish why your energies are low. Then take corrective actions.

ENLIGHTENED

ENLIGHTENED ENOUGH

*There is a tremendous sense of celebration and joy in finally
being able to join the family of buddhas. At last we have decided
to claim our inheritance, which is enlightenment.*
　　　　　　　　　　　　—Chogyam Trungpa

Shortly before his death, the Buddha was approached by a man named Subhadda who explained he wanted to join Buddha's order of monks but wasn't sure he was enlightened. The Buddha offered this guideline concerning enlightenment when he said: "Whenever the eightfold path can be found working itself out in a person's life, that person has realized the "phases of awakening." Here's the Buddha's path to enlightenment:

1. Right view
2. Right thought
3. Right speech
4. Right action
5. Right livelihood
6. Right effort
7. Right mindfulness
8. Right concentration

Evidently Subhadda was applying the eightfold path to his daily life because the Buddha welcomed him into the order of monks. He was enlightened enough. If you're seriously following that path, the Buddha would approve and say you are enlightened enough.

ENVIRONMENT

BUDDHIST ENVIRONMENTAL PROTECTION
*The wasteful consumption of natural resources and
destruction of ecology are caused by humankind's
psychological craving for convenience and wealth.*
　　　　　　　　　　　　—Sheng Yen

Buddha placed great emphasis on protecting the environment. One of his many teachings about respecting Mother Earth had to do with grasses, specifically, that we should not harm the grass and trees, but regard them as the home of sentient beings.

The next time you mow your lawn, pay attention to what's going on in the grass. You will find, as I have found, that all sorts of small beings flee the wrath of the coming mower—spiders, geckos, toads and many varieties of insects. Lawn mowing disrupts and destroys their living space.

Though completely ceasing lawn mowing would likely bring problems from neighbors, consider this: try mowing less often!

The Buddha loved nature and spoke out protecting the environment more than 2500 years ago. Here are some things to consider about the Buddha, his life and his focus on the environment:

He was reportedly born at Lumbini Garden;

Engaged in spiritual practices in the forest;

Gained enlightenment under a tree;

First began teaching at Deer Park;

His first "monasteries" were gardens and forests (Jeta Grove, Bamboo Grove, Amravana Garden);

Required all monks to spend the monsoon season in retreat rather than walk from village to village teaching. He did this to protect new grasses, plants and shrubs which emerged during the monsoon rains and would be easily damaged when trampled upon.;

He died between two trees near Kusingara;

Buddha encouraged his disciples, to spend the night outside under trees, to regard that place as his home and take loving care of it.

To this day, Buddhists great place emphasis on protecting the environment not only for humans but for all sentient being, for all plants, for all trees, for all lakes, rivers and streams. Join them in caring for the planet.

EXPANSION

EXPANDING KINDNESS

Kindness should become the natural way of life,
not the exception.

—Buddhist proverb

Generally, most people try to be kind to those they know. However, kindness needs to be greatly expanding and inclusive of every person we come into contact with. Here's an insightful example shared by a man who was on a business trip in China. He wrapped up his meetings and came home early in order to attend a birthday celebration for his mother-in-law. No one was expecting him, so as a joke he dressed himself as a waiter and began serving at the large, elegant party. His costume was perfect: hair slicked down under a cap and wearing the uniform of a server, he showed guests to their tables, poured drinks, carried and offered hors d'oeuvres.

Though he was in a full room with over 100 people, most of whom knew him well, not one person recognized or realized it was him. Later he told a friend "the surprise was that they didn't recognize me but the shock was they never even noticed me."

His experience raises the question: do we really see and notice the people whom we encounter in our daily lives: waiters, servers, baristas, clerks, laborers, receptionists, etc. Along with our family and friends, whom we see and greet warmly, we need to up our game and do the same for the people we can easily take for granted. This is one effective way of making kindness a natural way of life, not the exception.

F

FEAR

THE END OF FEAR

Caution yes! Fear no!
—Victor M. Parachin

A person strongly grounded in Buddhism exhibits little or no fear. There are several reasons for the absence of fear.

The law of karma which is not fate, nor is it an omnipresent power judging an individual issuing punishments and rewards. Rather, karma is a natural cosmic event arising from one's actions. Good actions, good words, good thoughts and a good mind, all of which characterize a Buddhist lifestyle, result in good karma.

The law of impermanence. When a Buddhist experiences life's challenges and difficulties, he or she remains patient knowing that life is not static, that his or her difficult circumstances will change, ease and end. During a time of difficulty, a Buddhist will engage in ways of resolving the difficulty as much as possible.

The inspiration of the Buddha. Like the Buddha, his followers know they have the seed of perfection within. Thus, they do not depend on external sources for their protection and salvation.

Confidence in the teachings of the Buddha. Those grounded in Buddhist philosophy utilize the insights and tools they have learned knowing they can confidently deal with whatever comes into their lives.

Support of the community. Sangha or community is a vital component of a Buddhist life. The quiet support, encouragement, inspiration and instruction from the Sangha strengthens one on life's journey. A serious Buddhist may exhibit caution but seldom fear.

FLEXIBILITY

BE LIKE A BAMBOO PLANT

Bamboo is flexible, bending with the wind but never breaking, capable of adapting to any circumstance. It suggests resilience, meaning that we have the ability to bounce back even from the most difficult times.
—Ping Fu

Because the bamboo plant can survive harsh winters, blistering summers and fierce storms it is an important symbol of enlightenment in Buddhism. Like the bamboo, enlightenment requires persistence, strength, flexibility and adaptability. The presence of bamboo also creates a sense of quiet and peace while providing shelter for human and other beings. It is especially venerated in China, Korea and Japan where the relationship between Buddhism and Bamboo is tightly linked.

For example, many Buddhist temples grow and nurture the plant on their properties. In addition, some temples include the word 'bamboo' in their names. Various bamboo species are named after the Buddha such as "Buddha Belly Bamboo", "Mercy Buddha Bamboo", and "Arhat Bamboo." Buddhism has also inspired various wisdom statements around the bamboo plant:

Bend but don't break. Be flexible yet firmly rooted.
You can lean on a bamboo stick but not on a rope.
Like bamboo, be resilient and bounce back.
The higher the bamboo, the more it bends.
Commit to continuous growth.

Any time you face a major life obstacle, bring to mind the bamboo and its ability to adapt, adjust, survive and thrive. Do the same.

FOCUS

WHAT IS THE BEST WAY TO LIVE?

The sole meaning of life is to serve humanity.
                                        —Leo Tolstoy

"What is the best way to live" is a question of great interest in Buddhism. The answer to this question is direct and simple involving four related approaches.

First, focus on the present moment. That means right here, right now at whatever your are doing. The very present moment is the only one over which we have direct and immediate control. So rather than lament the past or fret about the future, live wisely and intentionally in the present.

Secondly, focus on your own life. Make time to grow and evolve spiritually. Practice the art of meditation so that you are in control of your mind rather than your mind controlling you.

Thirdly, focus on those who come under your influence—a partner, children, family, friends, students, colleagues. Offer them support, kindness, encouragement, love and compassion. Be a role model to them as someone who exhibits wisdom and lives skillfully.

Fourthly, focus on being of benefit to the wider community. Dedicate yourself to improving the welfare and happiness of all beings, especially those whom you encounter during the normal course of your day.

FORCE

THE DALAI LAMA AND A PARROT

Religions are not all the same. But what they all say,
what they're all in agreement about, is that there's something
very wrong with your spirituality if it does not result in compassion.
If it results in unkindness and hatred and violence and
belligerence, you've lost it.
                                        —Karen Armstrong

When the Dalai Lama was a little boy he was separated from his parents and brought to live in the cavernous Potala Palace in Lhasa, Tibet. Without his family and without children his age to play with, the Dalai Lama says he was quite lonely during his childhood.

However, he spent many happy hours walking through the many gardens on the estate watching animals and birds. One of those was a parrot whom a monk befriended. Seeing the parrot eating seeds out of the monk's hand, the boy Dalai Lama eagerly held out some seeds to the bird himself. But when the parrot ignored his outstretched hand, he indignantly threatened it by shaking a stick at it. "Of course, thereafter it fled at the sight of me," he writes in his book *Freedom In Exile*. "This was a very good lesson in how to make friends; not by force but by compassion."

Relationships—family, friends, neighbors, colleagues, acquaintances, animal companions etc.,—thrive in the presence of compassion, kindness, cordiality, and gentleness. However, those same relationships wither and shrink under threats, intimidation, harshness and cruelty. Today may be an ideal day to review how you are relating to the lives of others in your sphere.

FREEDOM

THE FREEDOM OF LETTING GO

Attachment is the root of suffering.
                                        —Buddha

A wildlife photographer working in Alaska witnessed a battle taking place on a river. As he walked along the short, he observed a magnificent, large Salmon leaping in and out of the water. It was enjoying itself in the warm sun. What the superb creature did not notice was a bald eagle soaring high above. The majestic bird's sharp eyesight was also aware of the salmon.

Totally oblivious of the dark shadow rapidly descending toward it, the eagle silently swooped in sinking its knife sharp talons into the salmon's back. Then a furious battle erupted. The fish flapped and swam desperately attempting to dislodge the eagle. At the same time, the bird flapped its six foot wings frantically trying to lift the fish out of the water. The eagle was able only to do so for a few seconds at a time before the fish was able to pull back into the river.

As the battle raged, it became obvious to the scientist that the eagle was growing tired but refused to unlock it talons. Finally, the salmon pulled the regal bird lower and lower into the water where its flapping wings were useless. Eventually, all the photographer could see was the white dome of the eagle's head slowly disappear into the river. Then the water's surface stilled.

Here's the sad part: to survive all the eagle had to do was _let go._ Unfortunately, he was attached, literally and emotionally to winning that battle. In refusing to let go, the eagle lost everything.

That story is a metaphor about our own attachments. How often do we sink our 'talons' into something or someone only to discover the attachment begins to sink us. We are far too easily attached to our expectations—We expect life to be good, fair, smooth, without changes and challenges. We expect that we will live "happily ever after." We expect that our friends will understand and provide the support we need.

Yet, life doesn't always cooperate and that's when it's important to let go and practice non-attachment. That means loving but not grasping, enjoying but not possessing, appreciating but not gripping.

We all need to remember to release and relinquish.

FRIENDS

WHO DO YOU HANG OUT WITH?

Having good friends is like being equipped with a powerful
auxiliary engine. When we encounter a steep hill or an obstacle,
we can encourage each other and find the strength to keep
pressing forward.

—Daisaku Ikeda

Buddhist teachers are universal in stressing that the company we keep, that the people we choose as friends, is vitally important. The technical term form good companions is "sattva" or "sattvic" people. This is an individual whose thoughts, words and actions are guided and infused with light, compassion, insight, wisdom, and emotional-spiritual intelligence.

The teaching of Eastern sages on this matter is so critical that they often advise going it alone or having no friends if one cannot find sattvic people to associate with.

So who are the kind of people we should have closest to us? The answer would include, of course, a guru, spiritual teacher, yoga instructor, meditation leader. Writer Simon Chokoisk makes some additional suggestions which include "your wise uncle or aunt Mavis. Don't have any of those? Try hanging out with babies. Newborns, imbued as they are with the fresh redolence of sattva, can remind you of your essential nature. No babies? As a last resort, consider the company of young animals such as puppies, kittens and the like. Through their innocent eyes, you can see directly into of their creator." His last comment is fascinating and explains why almost everyone is drawn to young animals. They remind us of our essential nature—goodness, kindness, innocence, compassion, light—the very kind of people we want to be and the very kind of individuals we wish to be closely connected with.

G

GENEROSITY

GENEROSITY BUDDHIST STYLE

The practice of the perfection of generosity means
giving material things, good counsel and/or protection
from danger, and doing so on the basis of a pure
and free heart.

—Dalai Lama 3rd

Buddhism recognizes four important types of generosity.

The first is material generosity. This one is obvious. We give material things—money, food, clothing, etc—to those who don't have enough. When we do this for others, we show them, very simply and directly, that we care about them.

The second is emotional generosity. This is when we share of our time and our emotions. When a friend receives a medical diagnosis of a life threatening illness, we present ourselves offering support. When a person we know has experienced the death of a loved one, we, again, make ourselves present and available to provide comfort.

The third is the generosity of good counsel. This kind of generosity is offered when we encounter people who are captive to negative emotions such as anger, hopelessness, despair, anxiety, depression, bitterness. The generosity of good counsel has to be administered very, very sensitively. It cannot come across as judgment; it cannot come across a lecturing. It has to be conveyed as friendship. as we try to help guide their minds and emotions to a more noble path, toward a more beneficial way of being a human. We offer them spiritual tools which have worked for us such as yoga, meditation, pranayama (breathing exercises), inspirational books and articles.

The fourth one is offering the generosity of protection from danger. Some ways people can and do give "protection from danger" include defending a Muslim American woman who is being verbally attacked for wearing her hijab (headcovering); rescuing an animal which is in an abusive environment; driving a homeless person to a shelter when the weather is dangerously cold, etc.

Consider two ways of reflecting on these four generosities: first, how and when have you benefited from any of these? Identify them and the person or persons who reached out to you and express gratitude for them. Secondly, how and when have you offered these generosities to others. Recall those individuals and times expressing gratitude that you were in a position to be of benefit.

GESTURES

SEVEN MEDITATION GESTURES

Quiet the mind and the soul will speak.
　　　　　　　　　　　—Ma Jaya Sati

The Nyingma branch of Tibetan Buddhism teaches that there are seven "gestures" involved when sitting for meditation. These can be useful reminders for those who already have a meditation practice but are also helpful to those who wish to begin sitting meditation. Here are the seven "gestures."

> *The first gesture* is the actual "sit." Using a cushion on the floor, take a comfortable three pointed posture. The buttocks form one point and the crossed form the other two points. This is the gesture of communication with the earth, strong, stable, secure.
> *The second gesture* is a straight but not rigid back
> *The third gesture* is placing the hands on or near the knees with hands down.

The fourth gesture is to lift the head up a little as if you were placing it directly on top of the spine.

The fifth gesture is to soften the eyes. Beginning with your forehead allow any tension to release. Communicate with your eyelids instructing them to relax. Allow your eyes to be either closed or remain partly open.

The sixth gesture is to bring the tongue to the roof of the mouth, the tip lightly touching just behind the front teeth.

The seventh gesture is to instruct the jaw and mouth to relax. Allow the mouth to remain slightly open so you can breathe equally through nose and mouth.

As you sit, allow yourself to feel tranquil and relaxed. Let your meditation be a time of self-nurture and nourishment.

GOOD

JUST DO IT!

Think not lightly of good, saying, 'It will not come to me.'
Drop by drop is the water pot filled. Likewise, the wise one,
gathering it little by little, fills oneself with good.
—Dhammapada 9.122

In ancient China, there lived a monk who meditated high up in a massive tree. No matter if the tree swayed in fierce winds and rain, the monk settled himself comfortably, high up in the branches. Because of this, he was nicknamed "Birdsnest" by local villagers. Many of these residents passed beneath the monk while hunting or while gathering wood in the forest, so they grew used to him. Some began to stop and share their troubles with Birdsnest. They liked the things he had to say, and soon Birdsnest become known for his kind words and helpful insights.

After some years, the monk's wise reputation spread throughout the province. Visitors from distant towns and cities hiked to the remote forest for advice. He became something of a Buddhist tourist attraction. One day the governor of the area, a spiritual seeker, traveled two days to visit Birdsnest where he found the monk sitting calmly up in the tree.

Looking up, the Governor shouted, "Birdsnest! I am the governor of this Provence, and I have come a great distance to speak with you! I have a most important question!" The governor waited for a reply but heard only the pleasant sounds of leaves stirring in the breeze. The governor continued, "This is my question, tell me, Birdsnest, what is it that all the wise ones have taught? Can you tell me the most important thing the Buddha ever said?" There was a long pause—just the soft rustle of leaves again.

Finally, the monk called down from the tree: "This is your answer, Governor: Don't do bad things. Always do good things. That's what the Buddha's taught."

But the governor thought this answer far too simple to have walked two days for! Irritated and annoyed, he stammered, "Don't do bad things; always do good things! I knew that when I was three years old, monk!"

Looking down at the governor, Birdsnest replied with a wry smile, "Yes the three-year old knows it, but the adult still finds it difficult to do!"

GRATITUDE

THE GENEROSITY—GRATITUDE CONNECTION

The practice of generosity is like this: we do whatever we can to benefit others without seeing ourselves as helpers and the others as the helped. This is the spirit of non-self.

— *Thich Nhat Hanh*

Seicho Seisetsu (1274–1339) was a Chinese Buddhist who traveled to Japan in order to teach Zen. Because he was an extremely popular teacher, his temple became overcrowded requiring a larger building.

So, one day a local merchant brought Seisetsu a donation. It was a bag filled with 500 gold Ryo coins, an amount approximating to $1,350,000 US dollars. When he presented the bag to Seisetsu, the teacher simply said: "Fine, I'll take it." Unsatisfied with Seisetsu's response, the merchant explained him: "You know that one person could live a whole year on just three Ryo but in this bag are 500 Ryo."

Seisetsu abruptly responded: "You already told me there was 500 Ryo in the bag." Again, the merchant said: "Even if I am a wealthy man, five hundred Ryo is a lot of money." Seisetsu asked: "Are you asking me to thank you for it?" When the merchant said "You ought to as it's a lot of money." Seisetsu simply looked directly at the man and said: "Why should I thank you? It is you, as the giver, who should be thankful."

Quite bluntly, the Zen master, Seisetsu, is trying to offer that wealthy merchant two important lessons about giving. First of all, he seeks to make the merchant more mindful about his life of prosperity. The very fact that the merchant could make such a large donation means that his basic needs have been more than adequately covered, that he is in a very fortunate life position and that it is he, who should be expressing thanks and appreciation. Secondly, the Zen master is instructing the merchant offer his gift with a more pure level of generosity. Rather than give with expectation of receiving something in return, the merchant should simply offer the gift of money without seeking personal benefit, appreciation, or public acclaim. It's all about mindful generosity.

GRIEVING

TEN WAYS TO GRIEVE MINDFULLY

The mind has the capacity for great things;
it is not meant to behave in petty ways.
　　　　　　　　　　　　　—Huineng

If you've recently had the unwelcome experience of a loss—the death of a good friend or family member or beloved animal companion, the ending of a significant relationship, or perhaps the loss of health, the ensuing emotion is grief. Even this bitter taste of life can be the occasion to deepen our practice of mindfulness. Here ten ways to grieve mindfully and process the pain skillfully.

1. Mindful breathing. Grief produces stress and when you are stressed there are physical changes such as increased heart rate, fast breathing, and high blood pressure. The shortest route to reducing this stress is to breathe deeply and slowly. When you breathe deeply, it sends a message to your brain to calm down and relax. This is one way to do this. Sit quietly and comfortably. On your inhale say to yourself "in"; on your exhale say to yourself "out." Repeat for five minutes or more.

2. Mindful thoughts. When grieving it's easy to let the mind gravitate toward negative, catastrophic thinking. However, it doesn't need to be that way. Rather than have your mind manage you and your feelings, flip the switch and manage your mind training it to think positively and optimistically. Whenever negative thoughts emerge replace them with positive ones. Move from "I can't" and "I'm not able" toward "I can" and "I am able."

3. *Mindful words.* Pay attention to the way you speak. Is your vocabulary positive and uplifting or does it tend to focus on the negative and pessimistic. Use words, phrases and sentences which build up, encourage, inspire and applaud yourself and all those you come in contact with.

4. *Mindful support.* There are individuals around you who want to be as helpful as possible. Be mindful of who they are. Don't hesitate to lean on them from time to time. Avoid the temptation to isolate yourself when you are struggling. Reach out and let someone touch you.

5. *Mindful action.* Take steps necessary to learn about and adopt new coping skills to help you through the hardest days. Perhaps you could research and read online information about loss, grief and recovery. This would be a positive mindful act.

6. *Mindful silence.* There is a time to speak there is a time to be silent. Honoring these two will bring balance to your life an experience. Mindful silence can involve spending time alone in meditation, prayer, reflection, contemplation.

7. *Mindful eating.* Grief disrupts appetite. Some grievers eat too little while others over eat. Practice mindfulness at meals. Be sure to mindfully eat fresh, healthy foods to keep your body strong during your grief journey. If preparing meals for just yourself is uninspiring, use this as a reason to invite company over for a meal or try a new restaurant with a friend.

8. *Mindful exercise.* To offset the shock and sadness of grief, engage in regular exercise most days of the week. Studies reveal that exercise is just as effective for reducing depression as are anti-depressant drugs. Even if you feel you can't possibly drag yourself out of bed, get up and get moving. Think carefully about an activity that appeals to you—hiking, biking, swimming, yoga, group fitness classes, dancing, kayaking—and do it.

9. *Mindful determination.* Grief doesn't allow you to rewind your life so it's important to find ways of motivating yourself to keep moving forward. This means cultivating a deeper determination, the will to overcome grief and regain the joys of living.

10. *Mindful possibilities.* As grief eases and days become lighter and

brighter, be mindful about your future, about your ability to move forward and reinvent yourself.

GUILT

GOOD GUILT

None of us like to feel guilty and certainly some of us feel it when we shouldn't.
But it's not entirely without its purpose.
Imagine a world in which no one felt guilty about anything.
—Maria Schriver

Though guilt is most often presented as a negative and destructive emotion, there is this neglected or hidden aspect about guilt: it's a vital component of a healthy conscience and the sign of spiritual sensitivity. This positive and constructive side of guilt which nudges us to offer an apology, make an amend, seek forgiveness, restore a relationship and clear our conscience.

Furthermore, good guilt moves us to accept responsibility for our actions and, as we do that, we develop a deeper humility. Three of the hardest words to say are "I am sorry." It is our pride, our ego which makes it difficult to speak say those words. Without the prodding of guilt we can deflect responsibility by blaming others, pretending no one noticed our infraction, and or simply justify our conduct.

When guilt emerges in your life, look at it closely. Pay attention because it's a signal to take a second look at what is going on. Recognizing and responding to the source of guilt with wisdom, maturity and compassion liberates us to live in a healthy relationship with others and with ourselves.

Then guilt becomes beneficial, not damaging.

H

HAPPINESS

DRIVE YOURSELF HAPPY

Go confidently in the direction of your dreams.
—Henry David Thoreau

Is it not possible that if you can drive yourself crazy, you can do it's opposite and drive yourself happy. This can be done and here are some ways:

Spend more time only with people who are good to you and for you; people whose company you truly enjoy;

Work less or work in a field you truly find fulfilling;

Read more. Read in areas which give you pleasure—fiction, non-fiction, self help, science, spirituality, history, biography. The sky's the limit. Just follow your interests;

Help others. Do this not out of obligation but out of compassion;

Simplify and lower your standard of living so you don't need as much income;

Nurture your important friendships;

Meditate. Yes, you have time for it. No, it's not hard to do;

Focus on the positive, not the negative. This is merely a matter of choice;

Smile more. Smile at everyone you meet. This doesn't take much effort and many studies indicate that simply smiling makes one happier;

Develop your spiritual side. Read inspirational writings, meet with a study group, join with others in spiritual practices such as prayer, meditation, worship;

Ask "why" from time to time. And, if you don't like the answer then make a change;

Live in the present, not the past nor the future. Be here now. Enjoy this moment, this day of your life.

Perhaps Henry David Thoreau was thinking about ways people could be happier when he advised: "Go confidently in the direction of your dreams."

HAPPINESS IS PERSPECTIVE

How you think about a problem is more important
than the problem itself—so always think positively.
—Norman Vincent Peale

It's likely you've heard it said that "happiness is simply a matter of perspective." It's also likely you're familiar with the phrase "look through life with rose colored glasses" which meaning viewing events positively. Here's an example which reveals just how true and how helpful those two statements are when it comes to dealing with life's events.

A Buddhist monk encountered two visitors to his Nepal monastery shortly after a monsoon downpour. The storms had transformed the monastery courtyard into a wide pool of muddy water. He and the other monks carefully placed out a path of bricks to serve as stepping stones to cross the courtyard.

One visitor approached the edge of the water, surveyed the scene with a look of disgust and complained about every single brick as she made her way across. Once on the other side, she looked back at the monk saying: "Ugh! What if I'd fallen into that filthy much? Everything in this country is so dirty."

A few moments later another woman came into the courtyard. Seeing the brick path, she stepped out saying "hop, hop, hop" as she navigated over each brick. Landing on the other side, she looked back to the monk and said: "What fun! The great thing about monsoons is that there's no dust."

Two people experiencing the same conditions but two completely different ways of responding to them. Happiness is a choice. No matter what trial or calamity has fallen into your life, do your best to put the accent on the positive, the optimistic, the hopeful. Life is so much easier when look through "rose colored glasses."

TEN SIMPLE WAYS TO BE HAPPIER

Happiness is a choice.

—Victor M. Parachin

1. Spend more time only with people who are good to you and for you; people whose company you truly enjoy;
2. Work less or work in a field you truly find fulfilling;
3. Read more. Read in areas which give you pleasure—fiction, non-fiction, self help, science, spirituality, history, biography. The sky's the limit. Just follow your interests;
4. Help others. Do this not out of obligation but out of compassion;
5. Simplify and lower your standard of living so you don't need as much income;
6. Nurture your important friendships; drop those which are toxic. That includes dysfunctional family members. You don't need them.
7. Meditate. Yes, you have time for it. No, it's not hard to do;
8. Focus on the positive, not the negative. This is merely a matter of choice;
9. Smile more. Smile at everyone you meet. This doesn't take much effort and many studies indicate that simply smiling makes one happier;
10. Ask "why" from time to time. And, if you don't like the answer then make a change.

Perhaps Henry David Thoreau was thinking about ways people could be happier when he advised: "Go confidently in the direction of your dreams."

HARMONY

TOO TIGHT OR TOO LOOSE?

*Happiness is not a matter of intensity but of balance
and order and rhythm and harmony.*
                                        —Thomas Merton

An ancient Buddhist text reports an encounter between Buddha and one of his followers, Sona. Though Sona had been faithfully practicing meditation and following other Buddhist teachings he did not see much progress in his life. He was considering giving it all up and returning to the comforts of his wealthy family. Becoming aware of this, the Buddha engaged Sona in this conversation:

"Tell me, Sona, when you lived at home, weren't you skilled at the lute?"

"Yes."

"What do you think, Sona? When its strings were too tight, was your lute well tuned and easy to play?"

"No."

"When its strings were too loose, was your lute well tuned and easy to play?"

"No, Bhante."

"But, Sona, when its strings were neither too tight nor too loose but adjusted to a balanced pitch, was your lute well tuned and easy to play?"

"Yes."

The Buddha went on to advise that energy used too forcefully leads to spiritual tightness and restlessness while energy which is too loose results in laziness. The answer was in the image of the lute where the strings were neither too loose nor too tight. Buddha recommended that Sona find the right balance in his practice for him to evolve naturally.

From time to time, it's smart to make an assessment of our own living. Are we trying too hard becoming rigid, hard, fearful, judgmental and angry? Are we not being disciplined enough becoming careless, lazy, unfocused? It's important to find the balance.

HEALTH

HEALTH ASSESSMENT

Our thoughts and actions can be deemed either skillful
or unskillful depending on whether they assist or hinder
better conditions for the future.
　　　　　　　　　　　　　　　—Seth Zuiho Segall

Most people are familiar with the modern wisdom statement, "health is better than wealth."
However, many merely think of health as the absence of illness and disease. Buddhism has an expansive view of health which involves the complete person—health of body, mind, and spirit. For that reason Buddhist texts consistently emphasizes moral and ethical cultivation. Here are five examples:

1. *One should love those who are virtuous and take delight when others perform wholesome acts. One should never be envious.* —Sutra on Auspicious and Inauspicious Conducts
2. *Praise a person's good deeds. Do not point out a person's faults. Speak not of that which brings a person shame. Listen to a person's secrets but tell no one.* —Sutra on Upasaka Precepts
3. *Always reflect on one's own mistakes but do not remind others of their own shortcomings.* —Sutra Vimalakirti
4. *Constantly review your own behavior but do not look at the shortcomings of others. Be harmonious and do not contend with others.* —Moon Lamp Samadhi Sutra
5. *Always speak kind words. Avoid negative or destructive speech.* —Sutra of The Ten Great Dharma Wheels

HEART

THE 84,000 TEACHINGS OF THE BUDDHA

Have a generous heart: be patient; act kindly;
cherish all beings; radiate love to all.
—Victor M. Parachin

Venerable Khando Rinpoche travels the world teaching. Often when other passengers see him in his Buddhist robes he is asked "what is a Buddhist?" He finds the question intriguing and has asked his teachers how they would respond. The best answer, he says, came from his father: "Don't you see? Gathering the eighty four thousands teachings of the Buddha in one point: a good heart and an honest heart."

That's now the answer Venerable Khando offers when he is asked "what is a Buddhist?"

It's the answer any "religious" person should naturally have when asked "What is a Muslim? What is a Christian? What is a Jew? What is a Hindu? etc."

However, the big disappointment with "religious" people is their absence of a good heart. When that's missing what emerges is judgment, intolerance, fanaticism, and persecution.

The qualities of a good heart are the opposite—kindness, acceptance, tolerance, openness, friendship. That's built into some common everyday phrases such as *have a heart...she wears her heart on her sleeve...a heart of gold...good hearted.*

As you move through this day in contact with a wide variety of people—family, friends, colleagues, neighbors, clerks, servers, even strangers, remember to exhibit a good heart.

RESTORING HOPE

Hope is important because it can make the present moment less difficult to bear. If we believe that tomorrow will be better, we can bear a hardship today.
—Thich Nhat Hanh

Hope is a vital ingredient for living. With it, no matter the challenges, a person can endure and overcome. Without it, no matter the comforts, a person can feel disillusioned and despairing. Here are five simple, quick, and effective ways to restore hope.

1. Identify one positive in your life today. Not ten, not twenty, not a hundred. Just one. That's a good enough start.

2. Plan something small to look forward to twice a week. The emphasis is on small. Sitting quietly in a coffee shop. Reading a book. Stroll through a park.

3. Get outside. You, like most people, spend 95% of your time inside. That adds to sad feelings. Spending time outside—regardless of the weather—is spirit boosting.

4. Recall one person who was kind to you, good to you. Just one. That's enough to jump start hope.

5. Meditate for three minutes three times a week. Not ten, not twenty, not a half hour. Get a timer app for your phone. Set it to chime, ring, ding at three minutes. During the three minutes simply say, as you inhale, *Breathing in hope* and, as you exhale, *Breathing out hope.* Three minutes and you're done. You'll immediately feel more hopeful.

That's it. Five simple ways to restore hope. If you do this every week, you will soon be one of the most hopeful, optimistic, joyful, happy, blissful, jubilant, peaceful, cheerful person on the planet.

Go for it. Get hopeful.

HOUSEKEEPING

DUSTING MINDFULLY

The little things? The little moments?
They aren't little!
—Jon Kabat-Zin

A teenage boy in Vietnam, Venerable Sumangalo, decided to devote himself fully to Buddhism becoming a monk. His teacher assigned him a duty to dust one table inside the temple daily. Sumangalo admitted that he did the task grudgingly feeling he didn't become a Buddhist monk for the purpose of table dusting.

When he finished the simple task of dusting the table, his teacher would come to inspect. Placing his hand in the remotes and innermost part of the table, there was, inevitably, some dust still remaining. He instructed the novice monk to clean the table again saying: "How can you become a good monk without knowing how to dust a table?" A repeat dusting produced perfect results though the young monk still didn't like the assignment.

Several weeks later, the teacher came to carefully observe him dusting making this suggestion: "When you are clearing away the dust from this table, think as if you are clearing away the dust within in you." In an instant, the young monk understood the deeper meaning of table dusting. From that day on, Sumangalo did his task mindfully: mindful of removing all the dust from the table *and* all the dust from his mind.

Let his lesson inspire you as you attend to routine housekeeping chores. Do them intentionally, mindfully and gratefully.

I

IMPERMANENCE

A LESSON IN IMPERMANENCE

Like a sandcastle, all is temporary. Build it, tend it,
enjoy it. And, when the time comes, let it go.
                                        —Jack Kornfield

Impermanence—the fact that everything changes—is foundational in Buddhism.

Buddha taught that everything which starts and rises is subject to ceasing and ending. We all age and die. No matter how badly we desire youth, there is no escaping aging and eventually death.

The key for managing changes is to remain balanced and not be thrown off by changing conditions. When a Taiwanese Zen Master was in his 70s, he was diagnosed with serious kidney failure and had to be treated by dialysis. Many of his followers, some very wealthy, offered to help him get a kidney transplant. "You are a great master and it will benefit us for you to remain alive as long as possible," was the logic they present to him.

He declined without hesitation insisting whatever kidneys were available for transplant should go to a younger person, not someone who was already old and nearing the end of his life. There are two lessons from this Zen master: First, he knows how to age gracefully, not devoting his dwindling energies to fight with reality. Secondly, understanding impermanence empowered him to face death naturally, peacefully and with balance. Everything is subject to change. So, why be surprised, shocked or stunned when an unexpected, unwelcome circumstance emerges in your life?

INQUIRY

LEARN TO ASK BETTER QUESTIONS

To get the right answers you have to ask the right questions.
—Victor M. Parachin

Any time we are hit hard by life's blow, it's natural and easy to ask:

"Why?"
"Why me?"
"Why us?"
"Why now?"
"Why is this happening?"

The problem with "Why" questions is that they only feed our dark side, fuel our anxiety pulling and us further down. There are better questions to ask, questions which can lift our spirits when we're feeling down.

Here are some of those:

What are the chances that one year from now, I'll feel no better?

What advice would I give my child or my best friend if he or she were in my shoes?

When I overcome this issue, how will I be stronger, wiser, deeper and even better for it?

If I were writing a screenplay of my life, how would I have the main character (me) turn this adversity into an advantage?

How has this difficulty revealed to me who my true friends are?

Who could I confide in who would make me feel a little better, a little more hopeful?

What do I need to do to keep moving ahead with my life?

Who can I turn to when I need to express and explore what's going on with me?

By mindfully moving from "why" to "what, how, and who" questions, it's highly likely that life will run smoother, better, easier and with more freedom.

INJURY

MINDFUL INSECT CONTROL

*Do not injure the beings living on the earth, in the air
and in the water.*

—*Yajur Veda*

An important ritual at Zen centers is cleaning. Novice monks along with experienced masters all take some time out of their day to clean, scrub, dust, and polish everything in the Zen center. That includes floors, furnishing, windows, altars.

One reason for that is, of course, the discipline of cultivating mindfulness. To have a spotless, Zen center involves intense focus. Many beginning monks are scolded and reprimanded if they clean carelessly and leaving any trace of uncleanliness.

However, there is another reason why Zen centers are adamant about cleaning and it has to do with the five precepts taken by all who commit to a Buddhist way of life. The first of the five is this: "I vow to abstain from taking life." This means that Buddhists commit to non-killing and this includes not only humans but all life including insects—cockroaches, ants, spiders, beetles, flies, etc., are not to be killed nor harmed.

The most mindful way to fulfill the vow to abstain from taking life is to keep a Zen center spotless. Insects generally come indoor to find food and water. In order to avoid their presence and to escape the temptation to kill an insects simply keep a room clean and they won't come in.

This attitude applies to our own homes and apartments. To keep insects away we don't need to use harsh chemical poisons. We merely need to adopt a very mindful attitude toward cleaning and do so regularly. When this is done properly, an occasional spider or roach can simply be escorted back outside. This can be described as mindful insect control.

INSPIRATION

FOLLOWING NOBLE FOOTSTEPS

Benefit from the glow of others. Light your
small candle at their flame.
—Victor M. Parachin

Here's a simple exercise to expand your mind and enlarge your heart. Make a list of ten great people who have inspired the world and transformed consciousness. For example:

1. Gandhi and non-violence.
2. Mother Teresa and love.
3. Dalai Lama and patience.
4. Martin Luther King, Jr. and civil rights.
5. Thich Nhat Hanh and meditation.
6. Gloria Steinem and feminism.
7. Winston Churchill and leadership.
8. Rosa Parks and courage.
9. Princess Diana and compassion.
10. Eleanor Roosevelt and social reform.

Each week for the next ten weeks, make one of the individuals from your list be your guide. Let that person be the focus of your meditation, your thinking, speaking and acting. This will promote the development and growth of their elevated principles in your life.

INTOXICANTS

WISDOM AND ALCOHOL DON'T MIX

I vow to refrain from intoxication that clouds the mind.
—Fifth Buddhist Precept

Those who seriously follow and commit themselves to the Buddhist path agree to five "vows": The vow to abstain from killing, from stealing, from sexual misconduct, from false speech and from intoxicants.

Of the five precepts, the one least adhered to among Western Buddhist practitioners is the last one which deals with intoxicants: to abstain from consuming alcohol and using drugs.

Simply sipping a glass of wine is so ingrained in Western culture that many who say they are Buddhist are not aware of the prohibition against consuming alcoholic drinks of any kind. Buddhist teaching states clearly that alcohol is a danger. Ledi Sayadaw (1846–1923), a prominent Pali scholar and Burmese Meditation teacher, is the author of *A Talk On Intoxicants*. There he outlines these as <u>*some*</u> pitfalls of drinking alcohol:

> It corrupts the heart;
> It leads to addiction;
> It weakens good character;
> It gives a false sense of peace;
> It produces unwholesome karma;
> It destroys the healthy state of the mind;
> It makes the mind vulnerable to evil forces;
> It inclines a person toward sensual pleasures and wrong view;
> It overwhelms the mind producing confusion, negligence, heedlessness.

Though the Buddhist prohibition against alcohol consumption of any kind may come as a surprise, the teaching is clear: you can't mix alcohol and wisdom.

J

JOY

HAVE EXPANSIVE JOY

Be a person who celebrates, sincerely and robustly,
the successes, accomplishments and joys of others
as if they were your own.

—Victor M. Parachin

Someone I know recently came into an inheritance. As other family members and friends learned of this woman's good fortune, they did not share in her joy but became resentful, envious and even angry.

In Sanskrit there is an interesting word for joy and that word is *mudita*. While it can simply mean joy, *mudita* is specifically used when our joy is sympathetic or vicarious.

Mudita is a joy which delights in another person's success, achievements, accomplishments as if they were our own.

Sadly, many people feel pangs of jealousy or resentment when good comes into the life of another person. For that reason, Buddhism offers ways to have *mudita*. The first is to practice, practice, practice being happy when others have good things come their way. Your best friend became engaged, be happy for him or her. A family member receives a huge promotion and equally huge salary increase, be happy.

The other way Buddhism offers is through mudita meditation designed to cultivate, deepen and make permanent appreciative joy at the success and good fortune of others. This meditation can be done by sitting quietly and thinking of a person or persons who have had some very good fortune come their way. Try to feel what they are likely feeling. Try to think the happy thoughts they have been thinking. Walk in their shoes and experience your happiness and joy for them.

Furthermore, mudita joy means celebrating and being happy at the achievements and gain of others even when we are facing difficulty and tragedy. Buddhism recognizes that our enemies of joy and happiness are jealousy and resentment. The antidote to those negative attitudes is to engage in mudita practice.

K

KARMA

GOOD KARMA OR BAD KARMA

Like gravity, karma is so basic we often don't
even notice it.

—Sakyong Mipham

The word 'karma' is commonly used and often applied erroneously resulting in confusing ideas about karma. Often people come to the conclusion that they "must have bad karma." They feel this particularly if they are unhappy with the quality of their living.

However, according to Buddhist teaching, all humans can confidently believe they have good karmic roots.

There are four reasons for this confidence:

1. The Buddha said, "to achieve human birth is rare." That you are alive and here is indication of good karmic roots.
2. The Buddha said, "to hear teachings of liberation from suffering is rare." That you are engaged in Buddhist practices—meditation, yoga, chanting, mantra, etc., is indication of good karmic roots.
3. The Buddha said, "to practice the dharma (teachings) is difficult." That you are on this path is further indication of good karmic roots.
4. The Buddha said, "to meet an illuminated teacher is rare." That you have access to teachers (either in person or via their writings) who have some degree of Self-realization is yet another indication of good karmic roots.

Therefore, follow your path with confidence that it will bring you happiness and benefit.

KINDNESS

THE TWELFTH COW

Generosity can come in many different forms.
We can be generous with our possessions, with
our time, with our emotions, with our talents,
with our wisdom and with our joy.
                                        —Hsing Yun

An elderly man who was the father of four sons called them together at the time close to his death. He verbally gave them his "last will and testament" instructing them to divide his property absolutely equally among themselves. The sons had great respect for their father and agreed immediately to his final wishes.

After his death, they began the equal division of his property, money, clothing and miscellaneous household items. That was the easy part. The difficulty of even distribution of wealth were the father's eleven cows. An equal portion would mean that each son would get two and three-quarter cows. As vegetarians and a family who practiced non violence, there was no way they would slaughter one cow for equal division. Furthermore, the cows were rescue animals that their father protected over many years and the eleven cows were a family. So selling one off and splitting the money was not an option.

One of the sons suggested they consult with a meditating sage who lived nearby in a cave. After hearing their dilemma, the sage responded immediately: "This is simple. I have one cow that generously provides me with milk. I will give you my cow. That way you will have twelve and can divide them equally."

This charming story invites two questions to consider today. First, are you the kind of person who could give away your "cow" to help someone? Secondly, is there someone you know who would willingly give you a "cow" to help solve a crisis in your life?

KRODHA

BEWARE OF KRODHA

Anger can ruin all good practices and it is not soon forgotten.
It is attractive neither in the present nor when viewed later as
something belonging to the past. When anger begins burning
out of control like a raging fire, protect yourself and do not let
it consume you. Like a thief this fire will take away everything
you have. There is nothing worse than anger.
—Sutra Of Bequeathed Teachings

Krodha is a Sanskrit word for anger and is considered a dangerous emotional and spiritual condition. *Krodha* recognizes that anger exists in evolving degrees, from ordinary annoyances and slights to intense rage, contempt, violence, intolerance, vengeance and hatred.

No emotion is more degrading and debilitating for a person than a mind burdened with the varieties of *krodha*. Buddhism teaches that *krodha* or anger is one of the three "poisons", the other two being ignorance and greed. Furthermore, in Buddhism there is no such concept as "righteous" anger or "justifiable" anger. This emotion is always an impediment to spiritual growth and evolution. It's a chain which holds us back from complete Self realization.

Those seeking both happiness and enlightenment must apply disciplined effort to prevent this emotion from appearing as well as developing a cure for this crippling spiritual disease when it does appear. Anger, when unchallenged, clouds the mind, creates illusions and delusions, wastes energy, intensifies negativities, and promotes chaos in one's life as well as the lives of those around.

L

LEISURE

BALANCING LABOR WITH LEISURE

Happiness is not a matter of intensity but of balance,
order, rhythm and harmony.
　　　　　　　　　　　　　—Thomas Merton

One of the reasons people are so stressed is because they are one-dimensional—all they do is work. Their labor isn't balanced by much, if any, leisure and pleasure. Buddhist monks are very productive. They have mastered the art of balancing labor with leisure adding enjoyment to the work. Here are seven ways Buddhist monks do that:

1. Exercise. They do walking meditation, make pilgrimages, practice martial arts and some monks even dance.
2. Music. They chant, recite sutras, play musical instruments.
3. Art. They paint, carve, practice calligraphy and copy sutras using an elegant script.
4. Tea. They have an elaborate tea ceremony sipping and savoring the various tea leaf flavors.
5. Flowers. They do flower arranging viewing it as an exquisite art form.
6. Practice. They meditate, study texts, listen to teachers and teach others.
7. Labor. They work at building monasteries, gardening, maintaining property, cooking.

What would your list of seven leisures look like? Can you even come up with seven ways you bring pleasure into your labor and into your life? If not, then take corrective steps.

LEARNING

LEARN TO LET GO

Letting go is the opposite of desire or attachment.
Think of it as generosity in the highest sense.

—Henepola Gunaratana

The first "Noble" Truth of Buddhism is this: life is complicated. Traditionally this first truth reads "life is suffering" meaning that every human experiences disappointments and heartbreaks of varying types. That results in pain but we humans add suffering to the pain by our resentment that life was unfair toward us. For that reason it's important to learn to let it go when unpleasant, unwelcome events come our way. Of course, this is not easy. Yet, with consistent practice, it can be done and is done by people every day. Here are some "let go" motivators to think about as you reflect on your own personal experience with pain:

Let go of all negative thoughts and ideas that you can't manage the challenge of letting go.

Let go of regret by reminding yourself that bad things to happen to good people.

Let go of fear and dig deep tapping into courage and confidence.

Let go of blame. It doesn't change anything and only builds resentment.

Let go of believing your life is ruined and that you are damaged. It's just not true.

Let go of worrying. Accept what has happened and take one step at a time to rebuild your life.

Let go of the need to be more and do more. Simply do your best, day by day.

Let go of despair. Trust yourself. Believe in yourself.

Let go of anger. It is a huge waste of energy and time.

Let go of any self-loathing or self-hate.

Remember, you can and will rebuild your life. It will not be the same as it was but it can still be good and meaningful.

LIFE

THREE WAYS FOR A HEALTHIER *AND* LONGER LIFE

Long life is welcome, agreeable, pleasant, & hard to obtain in the world.
                                    —Buddha

1. Fill your plate with plants. All scientific evidence points to this simple truth: *a plant based diet is healthier for your body in all ways.* And when a vegetarian diet is combined with exercise and non-smoking, your life span lengthens considerably. Compared with a meat centered diet, plant based eating offers far more fiber and antioxidants. Keep in mind the wisdom of this Chinese proverb: "He who takes medicine and neglects to diet wastes the skill of his doctors."

2. Do yoga to keep your back healthy. It is true that you are as "young as your spine is flexible." You're old when your back is stiff. One recent study found that people with herniated disks—including a large number with sciatica pain—who did yoga for 3 months had less pain and disability than those who received standard medical care. The ancient Greek philosopher Plato observed that "lack of activity destroys the good condition of every human being, while movement and methodical physical exercise save it and preserve it."

3. Let meditation be your medicine. Again, studies continuously confirm that regular meditation reduces blood pressure, boosts immunity, lowers stress and eases insomnia, compulsive eating and depression. "The gift of learning to meditate is the greatest gift you can give yourself in this lifetime," says Sogyal Rinpoche.

Remember, it is much easier and more pleasant to retain your health than to try and regain it after it's been lost.

LIBERATION

SELF LIBERATE YOURSELF

We practice to liberate ourselves from a burden—
the burden of a narrow perspective caused by craving,
aggression, ignorance and fear.

—Pema Chodron

Huineng (638–713) was the sixth patriarch in the Chinese Zen tradition. While traveling with his teacher, the two had to cross a river. In the boat, the teacher said to Huineng: "When I was unaware, my teacher ferried me across. Upon awakening, I ferry myself."

The word "ferry" is a significant one in Buddhism. To "ferry oneself" means to self liberate. While teachers can be very helpful, at the crucial point, self-liberation is ultimately something only we can do for ourselves. Furthermore, it is vital that we continuously seek to expand awakening and evolve consciously.

Then, the question arises: *how do we self-liberate?* Try these seven ways:

1. *Self investigate.* Study people. When you see their positive, noble qualities copy them. When you see their negative, adverse traits correct those in yourself.
2. *Fertilize gratitude.* Appreciate the many positives of your life. This will ensure that you remain open and spacious.
3. *Be generous.* Generosity eases suffering, softens injustice, and heals divisions.
4. *Embrace change.* This means keeping the option to change your mind, change your direction, change relationships which have run their course. Avoid remaining frozen in place.
5. *Expand compassion.* Include not only those who love you but those who don't, those who hurt you and harm you. Make connections with others through compassion.
6. *Deepen character.* Take advantage of your troubles and trials to grow stronger and deeper.
7. *Cultivate silence.* It is the source of our deepest self-awareness, self-knowledge.

LIMITATIONS

RISE ABOVE SELF-IMPOSED LIMITATIONS

*Always discriminate between what is real and
what is unreal, what is eternal and what is
transient. Shun the transitory and fix your
mind on the eternal.*

—Sri Ramakrishna

In the Vedas, India's ancient sacred texts and ones studied by the Buddha, a story is told about a pride of lions hunting when a young cub was separated from the group. Lost, he wandered along the banks of a river until he came across a herd of wild donkeys. They accepted him and embraced him as part of their herd. The lion learned to eat grass like they did; bray loudly like they did; and kick their heels like they did.

The young lion lived with the donkeys for many months. Then, one day, his pride came back on the opposite side of the river. There they watched the lion behave in ways completely unusual for a lion. They called him across the river. They asked him to look at his reflection in the water and then to look at the reflection of the lions and the donkeys.

Immediately he realized he was not a donkey but a lion. His pride asked him to rejoin them to become who he truly was.

That Vedic story urges us to rise above our limitations and embrace who we really are. Too often our self-understanding is impacted and inhibited by the grip of upbringing and culture. Explore yourself. Ask "who am I really?" Remind yourself that you are not your job, your title, your looks. Go deeper and explore the true nature of self. Tap into the reality that the divine essence within is the same as the divine essence of the universe. You are divine! Be mindful of that truth.

LOVING KINDNESS

LOVING KINDESS FOR ALL BEINGS

When you cherish others, all your wishes are fulfilled.
—*Thubten Zopa*

It's likely that the first person on the planet to be spiritual but not religious was the Buddha. He was skeptical of all magical thinking which often arises in religion and offered an alternative path. This is evident when a report reached him that one of his monks died after having been bitten by a poisonous snake. The monastic community was upset over his death along with the fact that they were in the custom of chanting snake mantras for protection from a bite.

Using their experience as a teaching moment, the Buddha said that reciting magical mantras of protection were ineffective. However, what was powerful and effective was to develop loving kindness and compassion toward snakes. Then they could be free of harm from bites. The Buddha taught them this loving kindness meditation to recite during their meditations:

> *For those without feet, I have love.*
> *I have love for all with two feet.*
> *For those with four feet I have love.*
> *I have love for all with many feet.*
>
> *May those without feet do me no harm.*
> *May none with two feet do me harm.*
> *May those with four feet do me no harm.*
> *May none with many feet do me no harm.*
>
> *May all beings, all living beings*
> *All who've come to be—one and all*
> *May they see every blessing.*
> *May not evil come to them.*

It's clear in his words, that the Buddha wants all who follow his path to expand love, kindness, mercy, compassion far beyond snakes and reptiles but to extend it to the nations of insects, birds, fishes, four legged creatures. Everyone and everything is included and worthy of love and kindness. Cultivating this mindset is the ultimate protection.

LUNGS

LUNG POWER

Your work starts with your lungs. Why with the lungs?
Why not with your arms? By controlling the motion of the lungs,
mind's movements come under control.
　　　　　　　　　　　　　　　　—Swami Rama

Many who live in the West don't breathe properly or efficiently. The result of inefficient and ineffective breathing results in a variety of issues—emotional, mental and physical. Emotionally we feel anxious; mentally we are unfocused and constantly seeking distraction; physically there is head, neck and back pain.

In the East, breathing properly and efficiently is an art form and one taught to enhance not only meditation and mind control, but for the lengthening of life. Eastern sages have noted that animals which take fewer breaths live longer live. For example, a mouse takes 95-160 breaths per minute and has a life span of 1-2 years; a horse takes 8-15 breaths per minute and has a life span of 50 years; a giant tortoise takes 4 breaths per minute and has a life span of 150 years; most human beings take 15-18 breaths per minutes have an average life span of 70-75 years.

Because the breath is so vital, both Buddhism and Hinduism offer a variety of methods for improving human breathing. One of the simplest yet most effective ways for maintaining good health, better mind management and emotional resilience is to practice equal breathing. That means making your inhalation the same length as your exhalation. As you do this, breathe longer, smoother, and slower.

Here's a simple way to develop equal breathing. Find a place to sit quietly. As you inhale comfortably but slowly, say to yourself "breathing in peace". When in the inhale is full and complete pause holding the breath for a second or two. Then as you exhale comfortably but slowly, say to yourself "breathing out peace". Initially begin by doing this for three to five minutes at a time. As you become more proficient expand the time to 15 minutes or more.

M

MANTRA

DO YOU NEED A NEW MANTRA

*Mantra meditation is not magic, but the results
can be magical.*

—Thomas Ashley-Farrand

In Buddhism mantras are used as part of meditation because they have proven psychological and spiritual powers. They are so useful that some meditation techniques use them exclusively rather than sit in silence.

Skeptics and critics sometimes question whether mantra recitation really has any effect. Yet, a key focus for Western psychologists and therapists is to help their clients change the "mantras" they use
in daily life because the phrases they repeat are self-limiting, self-defeating and self-harming. In their counseling practices they constantly deal with individuals who live their lives with repetitive negative mantras—*I'm a loser; I'm a failure; My life sucks; Life is too hard; No one loves me; I can't do anything right; I'm too fat; I'm not smart enough, I'm an addict;* etc. Literally, the list of such negative mantras is endless.

If you're one of those whose life mantra is characterized by incessant negativity, then do what Eastern sages have always done, flip the mental switch to the positive side: *I am able; I am capable; I am wise; I'm a survivor; I am confident; I am enough,* etc. In fact, these very kinds of phrases are idea ones upon which to repeat in quiet meditation.

Something just this simple can be life transforming because it brings self-compassion, peace, and a deep sense of well-being.

MEDITATION

MEDITATION BENEFITS

Meditation practice is not an exotic or out-of-reach approach.
It is immediate and personal, and it involves an intimate relationship
with ourselves. It is getting to know ourselves by examining our actual
psychological process without being ashamed of it.
> —Chogyam Trungpa

One of the most effective ways to develop mindfulness is through meditation. Along with cultivating more mindfulness, here are another dozen more benefits which come from meditation:

1. If your heart has been broken, meditation can be your greatest guide leading you to heal the pain and experience renewed happiness;
2. If you are a sick, meditation can restore your health or it can provide you with the insight to managing the illness more skillfully;
3. If you are depressed, meditation can create greater mindfulness freeing you to emerge from depression;
4. If you are an addict, meditation can give you the insight and the power necessary for you to take corrective action over a habit which has enslaved you;
5. If you are a busy person working in a fast paced, hectic job, meditation can ease the stress and strain while producing relaxation;
6. If you are one who lives with fear, worry and anxiety, meditation can lift you into a more positive, hopeful and confident mindset;
7. If you are quick tempered and prone to anger, meditation leads to mastery of emotions creating a clear, calm mind;
8. If you are a wealthy person, meditation will deepen the awareness of your good fortune and how to make use of your wealth for your happiness and for others;
9. If you are a poor person, meditation will help you release self-limiting beliefs and increase self-confidence;
10. If you are a negative thinker, meditation will help you change your thoughts and transform your outlook

11. If you are standing at a crossroads in life and don't know which way to proceed, meditation will help you understand your proper role in life and the best path to take you there;

12. If you are a person turned off by religion, meditation can give you a spiritual pathway in life without rigid dogmas, harsh doctrines and unreasonable beliefs.

Even a small amount of meditation can bring you large benefits.

AIRPORT MEDITATION PRACTICE

The art of meditation is a way of getting into touch with reality,
and the reason for it is that most civilized people are out of touch with
reality.

—Alan Watts

Whenever we fly there is ample waiting time which can be used productively for meditation rather than scrolling through a smart phone. Here's how to do airport meditation when traveling:

Enter the terminal mindfully, peacefully, unrushed.
Find a place where you can sit and observe (not stare).
Glance at the people walking by.
Begin to imagine and understand that many of them feel fearful, anxious, lonely, abandoned.
Some may be dealing with personal health issues or those of a loved one.
Build a sense of connection with these strangers by reminding yourself -we are part of a common humanity; we're in this together; we share similar hopes, dreams, concerns, anxieities.
Conclude by offering this loving kindness message to people walking by you.

May you be happy;
May you be healthy;
May you be safe;
May you be free of suffering.

MENTAL

PRACTICING MENTAL DISOBEDIENCE

Our minds possess the power of healing pain and creating joy.
If we use that power along with proper living, a positive
attitude, and meditation, we can heal not only our mental
and emotional afflictions, but even physical problems.
                                            —Tulku Thondup

It's always good to review this questions for yourself: "Am I managing my mind or is my mind managing me?" Then, consider this highly effective way to become the manager of your mind—practice mental disobedience. Here's how that works:

If the mind says, "I'm going to eat some donuts" say to your mind "I will not cooperate with you today!"

If the mind says, "Instead of going to meditation tonight, I'm going to stream a movie" say to your mind "I will not cooperate with you today and will go to meditation."

If the mind says, "I must have a drink after work," say to your mind "I will not cooperate with you today and will spend time with spiritual friends at yoga."

If the mind says, "I need to scroll through my social media and email," say to your mind "I will not cooperate with you today and will take that time to meditate."

If the mind says, "I want to buy (whatever)," say to your mind "I will not cooperate with you today and see how I feel about that another time."

Through the mental disobedience, you will gradually shape the mind to become your servant, not your master. It's a positive and powerful way to help you break negative habits, remove unhealthy behaviors and eliminate self-defeating patterns.

MERIT

WHAT REALLY HAPPENS WHEN DREAMS COME TRUE

We benefit from virtues and suffer from vices.
                              —Victor M. Parachin

More and more people seem to be buying lottery tickets and a few of them win big. Interestingly, within a few months those same winners often describe their "good fortune" in negative ways such as: "The drama never ends." "I wish I'd torn the ticket up!" "The money is a curse." "I had to change my whole way of life and didn't like that." In addition to winning a lottery, there are those who also come into a "windfall" via inheritance or a payout from a law suit. Again, the same disappointing issues arise.

Buddhist wisdom addresses that kind of "sudden wealth" issue which through the story of a poor man in Taiwan who bought a lottery ticket with the few pennies he'd saved by scrimping on food. When he learned his ticket matched the winning number he was thrilled and decided to wait a few weeks before claiming the prize in order to avoid publicity. Wanting to keep his winning ticket safe, he hid it inside the walking stick he used because of his injured leg. One day while crossing a river, he realized that once he collected his money, he could afford medical care to restore his injured leg and would no longer need the cane. So, he threw his walking cane into the river and watched the currents carry it far away.

Here's the interpretation of that story: though the man did win a lottery, he did not have the "past merit" to manage the fortune. Navigating ourselves successfully through any event which generates a major life transition for us is dependent upon wisdom and skill cultivated long before the issue emerges. If we've neglected developing maturity, strengthening the mind and establishing the ability to face life with balance and equanimity, then we will be poorly equipped to deal with emerging issues. We have not created sufficient "past merit" to manage our life.

MINDFULNESS

THE BUDDHA, A KING AND MINDFUL EATING

People who always keep their hearts and minds calm and
know the right amount to eat experience few pains, age gracefully,
and live long lives.

—The Buddha

In the ancient Indian province of Kosala, the king invited the Buddha to visit and dine with him. A lavish was prepared for the two men. Having eaten until his stomach felt completely full, the king visibly displayed discomfort and heaved a great sigh. Seeing this, the Buddha offered him these words of advice: "People who always keep their hearts and minds calm and know the right amount to eat experience few pains, age gracefully, and live long lives."

Hearing this, the king reflected deeply on this teaching and began to repeat the sentence before each of his meals: "People who always keep their hearts and minds calm and know the right amount to eat experience few pains, age gracefully, and live long lives." Gradually he reduced the amount he ate and became the beneficially of few pains, graceful aging and the gift of a long, healthy life.

Though this was a legendary exchange between the king and the Buddha took place thousands of years ago, the Buddha's wisdom continues to be relevant today. When it comes to eating, too many people are at the mercy of their food lust. That is the reason why restaurants which advertise—"all you can eat"—are enormously popular. People eat mindlessly and over consume. This results in a wide array of health problems.

Today, it is important to remember the Buddha's teaching, "People who keep their hearts and minds calm and know the right amount to eat," and recall it prior to eating meals. Here are three ways to apply this wisdom and eat mindfully.

1. Eat only when you are hungry. Be sure that your previous meal has been fully digested before beginning another meal. Know the difference between true hunger and food desire.
2. Eat the right quantity for your gender, age, size. A good rule to follow is to have your stomach 1/3 full of solids, 1/3 full of liquid and 1/3 empty.

3. Eat in a comfortable place and at a comfortable pace. Eating a sandwich while driving your car is a negative dining experience. The same is true of eating while continuing to work. Your body needs an uplifting, peaceful, quiet environment to properly digest food. Make this available.

MIDDLE WAY

THE BUDDHA ON POWERING THROUGH

The Buddha's message was simple yet profound. Neither a life of self-indulgence, nor one of self-mortification can bring happiness. Only a middle path, avoiding these two extremes, leads to peace of mind, wisdom, and complete liberation from the dissatisfactions of life.
—Bhante Gunartana

In ancient India, a popular musical instrument was the zither, a flat stringed instrument played while resting on a musician's lap. The Buddha had a young disciple called Sona who was a fine zither player. Though Sona came from an affluent family, he abandoned the comforts of home to embrace the Buddha and his teachings.

He was extremely disciplined and faithful in practicing the teachings but soon became frustrated because he saw little improvement in his life and felt he was not much closer to the awakening the Buddha experienced. Rather than give up, Sona increased his ascetic practices eating very little, sleeping only three or four hours a day and spending the remaining time in meditation. He became emaciated and was frequently sick. Essentially Sona was "powering through" his practices.

Hearing about his, the Buddha visited his young disciple. Knowing that Sona was an exceptional zither player, he used the musical instrument as a teaching tool.

"Sona, you cannot produce good music on the zither if the strings are too tight, can you?"

"That is correct," Sona said.

"Sona, at the other extreme, you cannot produce good music on the zither if the strings are too loose, can you?"

Again, Sona agreed. So, the Buddha asked him: "What is the best adjustment of the strings to play beautiful music?"

"It is vital to tune the strings properly so they are neither too tight nor too loose," he said.

With that answer, the Buddha made this application: "Sona, you should realize the practice of the way which I teach is exactly the same. If you are too tight, extreme in your practice, you will strain your mind and become too tense. However, if you relax your approach too much, you will be overwhelmed by laziness. You must strike a balance, a middle path in your practice of the way as well."

This is an important lesson to all of us about "powering through". Sometimes it's necessary to do that but most often, we are far too hard on ourselves. We aren't powering through as much as we are punishing ourselves. Remember the middle way of the Buddha.

MIND

HEALING THE MIND

Our minds possess the power of healing pain and creating joy.
If we use that power along with proper living, a positive attitude,
and meditation, we can heal not only our mental and emotional
afflictions, but even physical problems.
—Tulku Thondup

It is worth nothing that most humans devote a great deal of time and money toward keeping the body healthy. We wash it and keep it clean; we clothe it for warmth and protection; we engage in physical exercise to maintain its strength and health; we see a physician when the body is sick and take the appropriate medicine.

And, it is also worth nothing that most humans are not nearly as proactive and careful about keeping the mind healthy. We seldom take time to think about the mind and what can make it sick, unhealthy, and left in a fragile state.

The mind, just like the body is adversely impacted by disease, diet and neglect. Diseases which weaken the mind are emotions such as anxiety, anger, fear, grief, sadness, insecurity, greed, jealousy. Diet which weakens the mind comes from the images we allow ourselves to read and to view: violence, cruelty, assaults, bloodshed, and other inhumane acts. Neglect— not paying attention and not working with the mind—also contributes to an unhealthy mind.

Those are the reasons why the Buddha placed so much focus upon the mind. Buddhism consistently challenges us to ask ourselves these types of questions:

What is the state of my mind?
Do I manage my mind or does my mind manage me?
Am I aware of my habitual reactions to my environment?
Is my mind primarily shaped by negative of positive emotions?

According to the Buddha, there is a 'cure' for a mind which is malfunctioning and that is meditation. The traditional Sanskrit and Pali terms for meditation—samādhi, dhyānā and bhāvān—simply mean bringing attention to the mind in order to know it, shape it and free it so that the mind becomes an invaluable ally rather than a powerful adversary.

MENTORS

LEARNING FROM OTHERS

Study people. When you see their positive qualities, copy those into your life. When you see their negative qualities, correct those in yourself.
—Victor M. Parachin

The Dalai Lama, leader of Tibetan Buddhists, tells of reading the biography of a seventeenth century lama named Tsele Rangdrol. In the book, he learned that Tsele Rangrol chose to give up eating meat, never accepting offerings for teaching and refusing to travel by horse as he considered this animal abuse.

Those actions inspired the Dalai Lama to do something similar. He decided not to accept offerings when he gave lectures requesting that all offerings and ticket fees be used for the organizers' expenses. The Dalai Lama also asked that all left over money be donated to a charity.

In your journey toward mindfulness consider reading about others whose lives inspire you to move in that direction. Read biographies about that person. Collect writings by that individual reading them carefully. Study their diaries and journals. In so doing you will create for yourself a powerful mentor and source of daily inspiration. To learn from others we have to pay attention to others, we have to be mindful of them—their thinking, their actions, their very lives.

By paying attention like this, an American learned a powerful life lesson. At the time he was hosting a Tibetan Buddhist monk who was giving lectures in New York City. As they used public transportation to travel from one speaking engagement to another, the American said they could save ten minutes by making a train transfer at Grand Central Station. When they got off the train, the Tibetan monk saw a bench and sat down. His host asked, "What are you doing? We need to keep moving!" Calmly, the monk said, "I thought we should enjoy the ten minutes we saved." This proved to be an important learning moment for the American who, like most Westerners, seldom takes time to slow down the pace of daily life.

MIND

STRENGTHENING THE MIND

Whether we are happy or sad depends on the mind.
When we are faced with adversity we need to know how
to look at the situation from a different perspective or approach the
problem from a different angle. As long as we are able to change our
minds, no problem is insurmountable.

—Hsing Yun

A popular teaching story in Buddhism is about a powerful, ferocious lion. This massive creature liked to vary his diet by eating, in turn, one from all the kinds of beasts of the field. One day he made the decision to eat a rabbit. Capturing one, the lion, looking sorrowfully at the small animal said: "You make a poor meal for me today. You're hardly worth eating and are so small you will hardly satisfy my appetite. Actually, there's very little use in eating you."

The rabbit answered: "Do please condescend to eat me; I have just had a narrow escape from being eaten by an animal as fierce as you."

Angered at the invasion of his territory by another fierce creature, the lion demanded, "Where is this animal which is as mighty as myself. Take me to it!" The rabbit led the lion away to a well, and told him to look down. Peering down into the water, the large creature saw another lion. Not realizing that it was merely its own reflection, the lion, raised its mane, roared loudly and showed its teeth. Then the lion leaped into the well to fight his rival and drowned.

This story is a lesson about the importance of developing powers of the mind. When the mind is focused, as it was for the small rabbit, one can overcome and deal effectively with a seemingly more powerful adversary.

MIND MANAGEMENT

THE IMPORTANCE OF MIND MANAGEMENT

The mind is the source of both our suffering and our joy.
Meditation— taming the mind—is what gets us from
one to the other.
                                        —Melvin McLeod

Your mind can be a supportive friend or a discouraging enemy. Your mind can let you see what is positive in your life or it can let you focus on the negatives. Everything depends upon whether you manage your mind or allow it to manage you.

Allow yourself learn from an experience which took place at a Buddhist monastery in Thailand. In the 1970s a young man named Peter Betts living in London, England was eager to pursue a spiritual path for his life. So, doing what many Westerners did in that decade, he made his way to Southeast Asia ending up in Thailand. Eventually, he would become a Buddhist monk in the Thai Forest Tradition but it wasn't easy and his path was filled with discouraging times.

One of those came early in his journey. He had recently joined a monastery and long with long daily rounds of meditation, the monks also worked hard physically maintaining the grounds and erecting buildings. Betts tells of a time when he and the other monks were instructed by the abbot to build larger main hall on the grounds. When the project was complete there was a huge pile of earth left over so the abbot asked them to move it to another location because it didn't look good where it was.

That task took many monks three whole days of hard work from nine o'clock in the morning until nearly ten pm with few breaks in the labor. When it was done, they were pleased with their effort. However, the abbot was called to another monastery for a few days. In his place, the deputy abbot came to the monks and said he believed they'd moved the earth into the wrong location and asked them to move it again. Once more this took three very long, tiring days in the Thailand heat.

The following morning their abbot returned and said: "Why did you put the earth in that spot when I asked to put it over there" he said pointing to the location. So for another three very long, tiring days, the monks relocated the pile of earth again.

By this time Betts was becoming extremely resentful and angry. He said that because he was a Westerner in an Eastern monastery he could swear in English without anyone understanding. As he pushed his wheelbarrow, he was uttering curses in English. However, from his body language they knew he was upset and angry.

One monk came up to him and said something which not only ended his frustration but transformed his mind. The monk, speaking in broken English, gently said to him: "Pushing the wheelbarrow is easy; how you think about it is what makes it hard." Hearing those words resonated immediately with Betts. He realized that he was indeed amplifying his difficulty, turning his problem into a disaster and had moved from trauma to drama. As soon as changed his mindset he found it was rather easy to push the wheelbarrow. In fact, he says it felt much lighter, he enjoyed the fresh air, and he enjoyed the company of his fellow monks that day.

Take that bit of wisdom: "Pushing the wheelbarrow is easy; how you think about it is what makes it hard," and insert into any difficult life issue. Some examples:

Being unemployed isn't difficult; how I think about it is what makes it hard.

Being single isn't difficult; how I think about it is what makes it hard.

Being married isn't difficult; how I think about it is what makes it hard.

Being disabled isn't difficult; how I think about it is what makes it hard.

Being poor isn't difficult; how I think about it is what makes it hard.

MINDFULNESS

TUNING OUT OR TUNING IN?

*Through mindfulness, we avoid harming ourselves
and others, and we can work wonders.*
— Thich Nhat Hanh

In ancient China there lived a very poor villager who made money selling vegetables at the local market. This involved great effort on his part. Rising early each morning, he would go into his small garden to pick the vegetable and fill a huge sack which he put on his back. Then he walked several miles to the village market.

One day, feeling empathy for the poor villager, someone offered to loan him a horse. The villager accepted and was amazed at how much he could load onto the animal and take to the market.

He'd never ridden horse before and didn't know how to mount the animal so he used a ladder to get on the creature.

Once he was comfortably seated on the animal's back, he gave the command for the horse to "go" and was stunned when the huge creature bolted faster than he ever imagined. His vegetables flew everywhere and he slipped upside down barely managing to encircle his arms and legs around the horse's neck.

As the horse raced through the village, a friend saw the man and shouted to him: "Where are you going in such a hurry?"

The man replied: "I don't know! Ask the horse!"

In this story, the horse symbolizes mindlessness. Many people are riding rapidly on horse without knowing where they are going. They move through life following habitual patterns and then wonder why their lives appear to be out of their control.

The antidote is to stop, to pay attention, to be mindful of patterns, habits, and conditioned reactions which do not serve us well.

In other words, we have to hold the reins of the horse and control it; we need to manage life rather than continue to allow life to manage us.

Today resolve to begin moving from inattention to attention, from reaction to response and from the habitual to the intentional.

N

NEEDS

HOW BAD IS YOUR LIFE, REALLY?

Always remind yourself that if you have food, clothing and shelter, your basic needs are met.
—Victor M. Parachin

The 14th Dalai Lama tells a story from his childhood saying that his mother was "undoubtedly" the kindest person he'd ever known and then tells a time of terrible famine in neighboring China. As a result many starving Chinese crossed the border into Tibet seeking better conditions. One day a couple appeared at his home, carrying in their arms a dead child.

They asked his mother for food which she readily gave them. Then, she pointed at the dead child offering to help bury it. This additional kindness was conveyed through hand gestures as language was a barrier. When the starving couple eventually understood what the Dalai Lama's mother was asking, they shook their heads and made it clear they intended to consume the corpse. The Dalai Lama's mother was horrified and immediately invited the couple in and gave them all the food she had stored in her kitchen before regretfully sending them on their way.

As anguishing and agonizing as that true story is, it prompts all of us to ask this question: "how bad is my life, really?" It is really that bad just because you've been downsized? Is it really that bad just because you've had a relationship break up? Is it really that bad just because you don't feel you're doing as well as others are? Is it really that bad because you're an addict? Is I really that bad just because you're in debt? Is it really that bad just because you've had a personal or professional setback? Is it really that bad just because...?

Compared to the couple with the dead baby, our lives are actually quite stable, good and full of potential.

P

PATH

FOLLOWING YOUR PATH

*No one else can walk your path for you. No one else can
achieve enlightenment for you. All anyone can do is to point
you in the right direction and allow you to do the rest.*
—Wu Wei

Zen master Gutei often raised his finger when he answered questions
and when he taught. A new, young novice disciple began to imitate him.
Each time Gutei raised his finger, the young man raised his finger as well.
Other monks began to laugh.

One day, Gutei, noticing what the young disciple was doing, grabbed
the boy's hand, whipped out a knife, cut the finger off and tossed it away.
Understandably, the young disciple began to walk away howling with pain
and humiliation.

"Stop!" yelled Gutei. The boy stopped and looked at Zen master
Gutei through his tears. Once they both made eye contact, Gutei raised his
finger. Out of habit, the boy raised his finger suddenly realizing it wasn't'
there. He hesitated a moment, smiled, bowed in gratitude.

When people first hear this story, they ask: "Did that really happen?"
No one knows but it would not be out of keeping for ancient Zen masters
to respond in surprising and shocking ways to a disciples behavior.

What is important, however, is what transpired in the young disciples'
life. Obviously, he gained an insight, significant enough that it erased his
humiliation over the incident.

Gutei was teaching the novice disciple, in the most radical way
possible, that one can't imitate enlightenment, Self-realization, Higher
consciousness, etc. "Walk your own path" is the lesson he was conveying.
It is useful to study with others, learn from realized masters, read deeply

but ultimately, the journey to enlightenment is unique to the individual. Imitating, copying, or emulating a teacher is simply a counterfeit approach, a forgery and will never lead one to the real experience of spiritual evolution and growth. Rather than copy another person's version of enlightenment, follow your own path.

PATIENCE

GIVE YOURSELF TIME

To become Buddhas, we need to practice patience.
There's no way to become a Buddha if we can't be
patient and tolerant.
                                        —Thubten Chodron

Anytime you make a decision to develop yourself personally or professionally, keep in your mind the image of a tiny tree seed. Then remember that it will take time for that seed to emerge from the earth, rise up, and stand tall. It's never helpful to start questioning yourself these ways:

Why am I not making more progress?
Why is this so hard?
Why is this taking so long?
Why are there issues?
Why can't I get past them?

It takes time for a seed to grow, so give it time. Quit asking yourself self-defeating, self-sabotaging questions. Instead, cultivate patience because if you don't, here's what will happen:

You will make poor decisions;
You will have wasted all the time you put into self-development;
You will end up feeling like a failure;
You will increase self-doubt and decrease self-confidence.

PERCEPTION

DON'T BELIEVE EVERYTHING YOU SEE

Whenever we perceive something, it is always filtered through our emotions, our desire, jealousy, pride, ignorance, and aggression.

—Cortland Dahl

Unless our minds and senses are well trained, many times we do not see reality clearly. Everything seen is filtered, shaped and altered by the causes and conditions of our lives. This Buddhist teaching is emphasized through a story about an elderly monk with a large following. Among his disciples was one who was becoming annoying. He "didn't get it" and was unable to understand Buddhist teachings Furthermore, when he didn't understand, he argued with the monk who, in turn, became frustrated with him.

One day the disciple asked for yet another one on one meeting with the monk. While he was thinking about how he could help this man, a tofu merchant came into the temple and saw the monk had a worried look on his face. "Venerable master, what is troubling you and is there any way I could help?" he asked. The monk explained: "I have a disciple coming to meet me today. He is stubborn and difficult to deal with."

Eager to be of assistance to the monk, the tofu merchant suggested he be permitted to meet with the disciple. "Even I have trouble teaching the disciple so how could a tofu merchant do any better?" he thought to himself. As he considered the request it occurred to him that perhaps another personality using a different approach could reach the disciple and help him learn. So he agreed.

The merchant asked to borrow the monk's robe, put it on and sat down in the temple to wait for the student. As the disciple entered the temple, he saw his teacher sitting and approached him holding all ten fingers up to the monk. When the merchant saw that, he responded with five fingers of his own. The disciple answered that with three fingers and finally, the merchant put out one finger. That made the disciple smile and he left with a respectful bow.

After arriving at his home, that disciple told his family and friends that the "elderly monk is indeed an excellent teacher because today he help me understand the Buddhist way very clearly." Asked how he taught, the disciple explained what transpired: "When I stood before him, I stretched out both hands to ask him how I could refrain from ten unwholesome actions. He held up five fingers, telling me to obverse the five precepts. Then I held up three fingers to ask him how to ride myself of the three poisons of greed, anger and ignorance. He answered with a single finger to tell me that having one mind and eliminating duality is the answer. He made everything so clear for me today."

As that conversation was taking place, the master monk asked the tofu merchant how the discussion ended so quickly. The merchant said: "Your disciple drives a hard bargain. As soon as he came in, he help up ten fingers to ask me how much for ten squares of tofu. I put out five finger to tell him five dollars. Then he held up three fingers indicating he would only pay three dollars. I became very angry with him and jabbed my finger out at him. This embarrassed him and left immediately."

This story is a reminder that we can't believe everything we see; that our perceptions are often limited and distorted by circumstances and experiences of our lives.

PERSEVERANCE

PERSEVERANCE POWER

The difference between a successful person and others
is not a lack of strength, not a lack of knowledge, but rather
a lack in will.
—Vince Lombardi Jr.

Most people want to be successful at something important to them— becoming an author, musician, artist, losing weight, exercising regularly, doing meditation daily, etc.

And Most people don't succeed in fulfilling their desires. Why? Because they don't really want it. They are more attached to the idea and simply don't give their dream the energy, commitment and drive to achieve it.

Knowing that this is far too common an issue with people, Zen masters would often test a person before accepting an individual as a student. Often the test was long and burdensome. In the Chinese Zen tradition the story is told of a group who traveled many miles from the south to the north in order to study with a master. The trip was not only lengthy and expensive but quite dangerous.

Upon arrival they were cold, hungry and tired. After knocking on the door to the temple, no one responded. They waited and knocked, off and on, for several hours. Finally after several days of no response, the group simply packed up and left in frustration with the exception of a man named Fayuan who remained committed. That night a monk opened the door and asked "why are you here?" Fayuan said "I have traveled many miles to come here and study with you." Without any explanation, the monk threw a basin of water on Fayuan and said "our teacher doesn't have time for someone like you. Go away."

Those harsh words didn't deter Fayuan who respectfully responded: "I have traveled thousands of miles from the south to be here. I will not turn back just because you douse me with water. I will remain and wait."

Impressed by Fayuan's determination, the monk allowed him to enter and work in the kitchen. At that time, China was undergoing a period of famine so food supplies, including cooking oil, were carefully rationed. One day Fayuan used some of the valuable oil to cook noodles for guests at the monastery. When the head abbot learned about this he sent for Fayuan reprimanding him: "This oil is the property of the Temple. How could you be so careless with it. I insist that you repay the temple for the oil you used." Knowing Fayuan was in complete poverty and had no money to buy more oil, the abbot said: "If you do not have any money, you can leave your robe behind as payment and you must leave."

Still determined to become a monk, Fayuan decided to remain under the eaves of the temple roof. His plan was to collect alms from entering visitors and thereby repay the Temple for the oil. A few weeks later the abbot learned Fayuan had been camping outside the Temple so he called for him and asked him to pay the temple rent for his spot under the roof.

After several other such tests to assess how badly Fayuan really wanted to learn the Buddhist way, the abbot became impressed with Fayuan's persistence and honesty. Eventually, the abbot named Fayuan to be his successor.

Ask yourself these kinds of motivational questions: *How badly do I want this? How much am I willing to sacrifice? Do I have it in me to stay for the long haul?*

POISON

FOOD POISONING

It is surprising how few people are aware that eventually good food can be harmful when prepared and served by one who is anxious or fearful or one whose mind is dominated by anger or resentment.

—Philip Kapleau

Several years ago we took a family vacation arriving at our destination in the early evening. My young sons and I went to a small sandwich shop near our hotel. There was only one employee, a young woman, who was on the phone shouting and arguing with someone with someone at the other end. It was a heated exchange. When she saw us, her customers, she hung up and with a flash of irritation, took our order making the sandwiches. I paid for the order but because of her emotional state, I tossed the sandwiches into a garbage bin once we were outside telling the boys we'd find another place to pick up food.

Buddhism understands that human energies interact and affect us. The negative vibrations of the person preparing food have the power to "poison" the meal causing those who consume it to experience, not nutrition, but reactions such as digestive issues, upset stomach, headache and other ailments.

It's that understanding which guides many Buddhist monasteries to select the community cook very, very carefully. After the abbot, the second most important person in a Buddhist monastic setting is the cook. The person chosen for this task is someone who is advanced in his or her practice, has a positive mind and who is emotionally stable, balanced.

So, keep this in mind when you are the cook. Do your best to be peaceful, relaxed, happy as you prepare nourishing food for yourself, your family, your friends.

POSITIVE

A POSITIVE LEADS TO A POSITIVE LIFE

How we think is how we will act.
—Victor M. Parachin

In the Jewish tradition there is an ancient story which is told about a man who came to a rabbi asking for help. "I'm sick and can't work," he explained. "My wife is also unwell and not strong enough to even take in laundry to make a little money. Because of our poverty, several of our children are sick and need medicine. I' don't know what to do. Could you possibly give us a little money?" he asked.

The good rabbi reached into his desk, took out some money and promptly gave it to the man.

Hearing about this act of kindness and generosity, a community member came to the rabbi that afternoon saying: "Rabbi, the man who came to you this morning saying he was sick, his wife was sick and that his children were sick was lying. None of them are sick."

Without hesitation, the rabbi smiled and said, "Thank God they're all healthy!"

Insert yourself into that story assuming the rabbi's position. Would that have been your immediate response?

Or, would you have felt deceived and cheated?

The difference in responses is simply how we train the mind. It can either focus on the negative or upon the positive. It can be trained to be either skeptical and dismissive or optimistic and helpful.

That's why the Buddha stressed the importance of training the mind to focus more on the positive rather than the negative. He taught that the mind can be our source of joy or our source of suffering. It's all depends on where your mind places the emphasis.

FOUR BUDDHIST POWERS FOR A BROKEN HEART

*The world breaks everyone and afterward many are strong
in the broken places.*
    —Ernest Hemingway

Sooner or later something happens which breaks our heart. Someone we have loved leaves us. A trusted friend betrays us. A child dies. An employer whom we have served faithfully, let's us go.

Sadly, some lives are filled with too many heart breaking experiences. It is when our hearts are broken and grief is mightily present that we need to utilize and develop these four powers of Buddhism.

1. *The power of superior understanding.* Cultivating the power of "superior" understanding. means remembering and putting into practice the Buddhist teaching of impermanence. Simply stated, impermanence reminds us that "this too shall pass." It is an undeniable truth of our existence that life is constantly in flux, changing and moving from good to bad and from bad to good. Recalling this principle will bring us the understanding and patience necessary to weather a tough time.
2. *The power of a strong will.* Perseverance and persistence are required to get through a season of pain and grief. Writing in 1911, James Russell Miller emphasized the necessity of will power: "Self-control is self-mastery. It is kingship over all life. At the center of your being sits yourself. Your seat ought to be a throne. If you are not in control, if there are any forces in your nature that are unruly, that do not acknowledge your sway, you are not the king you should be. Part of your kingdom is in insurrection. The strength of your life is divided. The strong man is he whose whole being is subject to him."
3. *The power of joy.* It's possible to experience joy in spite of pain. Doing this means choosing your perspective. Don't limit your life by opting only for sadness and unhappiness. Choose to do things and be with people who bring joy and happiness your way.
4. *The power of rest.* The pain and grief of a broken heart are taxing and exhausting. Whenever you find yourself physically, mentally, emotionally tired, allow yourself to rest, back off, ease up. This will allow your energies to return.

Q

QUESTIONS

TEN QUESTIONS TO ASK OF YOURSELF

*He who knows others is wise. He who knows
himself is enlightened.*

—Lao Tzu

Every now and then it's a good exercise to ask some soul expanding questions of yourself. Here are ten to consider this day. Look them over carefully; pause after each one allowing an immediate intuitive answer to come into your mind.

1. What am I doing to help others?

2. What is worth suffering for?

3. What is holding me back today?

4. Who do I love?

5. Do the people I love know it?

6. What part of my life needs a change?

7. How do I make others feel?

8. What makes me happy and come alive?

9. What can I let go?

10. What can I embrace more completely?

If there are responses you don't like, then view those as areas in your life which need closer examination, attention and transition.

QUIT

QUITTING ANGER

Every one of us feel anger at times, but it is an emotion
be wary of. Anger shrinks us and contaminates us, keeping
us poor and fearful. It kills love and keeps us distant
from other people.

—Christopher Hansard

To witness someone who successfully manages to quit anger, all we need to do is have a closer look at the Dalai Lama. He was born in 1935 and in 1950, when he was still a teenager, fifteen years old, he was installed as the leader of Tibet. It was a dangerous time for his country as China was a looming threat to his nation. So, at fifteen he was the political and spiritual leader of his people trying to navigate a path with China. That's a lot of pressure for an adult but he was in his teenage years.

In 1959, when he was 24, he was forced to flee his country because of the Chinese invasion and risk to his own life. He crossed the Himalayan Mountains in March when it was still bitterly cold eventually making to India which granted him refugee status. Absent from Tibet, the Chinese were ruthless in the destruction of temples and the arrests of monks, nuns and Tibetan lay people. Reports of atrocities came to the attention of the Dalai Lama regularly.

Years later he was interviewed by a reporter who asked: "In spite of all the damage and pain inflicted by China, you are not angry and repeatedly encourage Tibetans not to hate the Communist Chinese for what they did. How can you not be angry?"

His answer is inspiring and instructive: "What good does it to be angry? Anger doesn't free any of the Tibetan people. It doesn't stop the harm that is going on. It would just keep me from sleeping and from being able to digest my food. Holding a grudge would just make me bitter. What positive result could anger bring me?"

The next time anger rises with you, for whatever reason, pause to remind yourself of the Dalai Lama's observation: "What positive result could anger bring me?"

R

READING

WHAT YOU READ SHAPES YOUR LIFE

*When I get a little money, I buy books. If any is
left, I buy food and clothes.*

—Erasmus

The written word shapes and transforms our lives. One way to
understand Gandhi and the powerful, peaceful movement he launched is to
look at the books which he read. Here's a partial list of volumes important
to Gandhi and which shaped his personality and worldview:

A Plea For Vegetarianism (H. S. Salt)
The Kingdom of God Is Within You (Leo Tolstoy)
The Bhagavad Gita
Civil Disobedience (Henry David Thoreau)
The Yoga Sutras (Patanjali)
The Sayings of Mahomed (Abdulla Sohravorthy)
The Way of Zoraster (Sadi Sheikh)
The Sikh Religion; It's Gurus; Sacred Writings And Authors (Max Arthur
    Macauliffe)
Ethical Religion (William M. Salter)

Books shape lives.
What books are shaping your life?
To find out, make a list of the last seven books you've read.

RECYCLING

THE BUDDHA RECYCLED

Just as we get sick physically, the earth is sick too. When people are sick, they need to be treated and saved. When the earth is sick, it also needs everyone to care for it and save it. To save it, we must begin with environmental preservation.

—Hsing Yun

Starting with the Buddha himself, Buddhism has always been concerned about the environment and promoted living in harmony with the planet and its needs. Here are some of those ways:

The Buddha experienced his awakening outdoors beneath a tree;

He continued to meditate outdoors and often taught in natural settings;

The Buddha recycled. His first robe was made from discarded cloth he found in a village dump. There he gathered the material, cut it, sewed it and dyed it to make a saffron colored robe which is common among Buddhist monks worldwide to this day.

The first precept of Buddhism—to abstain from the taking of life—means giving respect to all living beings;

The Buddha established monsoon retreats because he didn't want monks walking and trampling new life forms which emerged during the rainy season;

Buddhist teachers have traditionally stressed the importance of protecting mountains, rivers and mother earth;

When the ancient Indian King Asoka became a Buddhist he applied Buddhist teachings to his government by planting trees, establishing animal hospitals, and offering only vegetarian meals out of the palace kitchens;

Buddhist festivals and celebrations often include releasing captive animals;

Right livelihood is one of the precepts of the Noble eight fold path which directs adherents to avoid jobs which harm the planet or hurt other beings;

Buddhism promotes compassion, kindness, happiness and non

violence applying these toward the planet and everything on it.

Like the Buddha, we each should continue to be mindful by looking
closely at our own habits and lifestyles which contribute to pollution
and depletion of natural resources.

REFRAMING

REFRAMING YOUR LIFE

*I don't know whether the universe, with its countless galaxies,
stars and planets, has a deeper meaning or not, but at the very
least, it is clear that we humans who live on this earth face the
task of making a happy life for ourselves. Therefore, it is important
to discover what will bring about the greatest degree of happiness.*
—Dalai Lama 14th

As a man walked past a construction site, he saw two bricklayers
about ten feet apart from each other, both laying bricks. The first man
looked lethargic, despondent, and morose as he laid brick after brick. The
second man, on the other hand, looked energized, upbeat, and inspired
as he did the identical activity. Curious about this difference, the passerby
approached the first man and said: "I'm sorry to bother you sir, but may I
ask what you're doing?"

The unhappy man barely looked up saying, "I'm just laying bricks."
The passerby thanked him then approached the second man, asking him
what he was doing. With great enthusiasm and a strong voice, the man
declared: "I'm building a great cathedral."

Two men doing the same job. One was "just" laying bricks; the
other was building a great cathedral. One man is disconnected from his
life purpose; the other has maintained his link to the deeper meaning of his
work. The difference between the two is vast and significant. That parable is
a powerful reminder about reframing your life in order to re-ignite passion
and purpose.

Reframing simply involves removing negative, self-defeating
thoughts and replacing with positive self-affirming ones. For example, if
you are in medical school and overwhelmed by the amount of information

you must absorb and memorize, pause to remind yourself how enthusiastic you became when you received your letter of admission to medical school. Relive those positive feelings and allow them to reframe how you see your task that day. That approach can be taken to any aspect or any time of your life when everything feels empty, monotonous, dreary, boring, meaningless.

REINVENTING

REINVENTING YOUR MEDITATION PRACTICE

Meditation is a long journey, not a single insight or even several insights. It gets more and more profound as the days, months and years pass. Keep meditating.
—Dalai Lama1 14th

If you're meditating with some regularity but not finding it as motivating as it once was, consider re-inventing your meditation practice rather than allow it to dwindle away and disappear.

Some signs that a meditation practice needs help include:

boredom
laziness
less desire to practice
finding excuses not to do it
craving—feeling there are no results
doubt—believing meditation isn't really useful

Rather than give it up, the above are indicators that perhaps your practice needs to be reinvented. For example, if you meditate alone, try out group meditation. If your practice is silence, switch to chanting or mantra recitation or candle gazing, guided meditation or sound meditation or using mala beads.

Buddhism teaches impermanence, meaning that nothing is unchanging and that includes your meditation practice. In fact, your very practice may be trying to move you into another direction in order to be a more meaningful practice. Just as you have changed over the months and years, perhaps your practice needs refining. Personal tastes change all the time—tastes in clothing, food, friends etc. The same may be true for meditation. So, don't hesitate to adapt and modify. This can be a subtle shift or one which is more profound.

RELEASING

THE FREEDOM OF RELEASING

People have a hard time letting go of their suffering.
Out of a fear of the unknown, they prefer suffering
that is familiar.

—Thich Nhat Hanh

In ancient India, villagers developed a simple and successful way to capture a monkey. A person would first find a ripe coconut, cut out a hole roughly the same size as a monkey's hand and drink up or drain it of the sweet milk. Then the coconut would be tied to a tree in the forest and, a small banana would be placed inside the coconut.

Before long, a monkey would discover that hollow coconut with a banana inside. It would reach in, grasp the fruit and try to pull it out. However, the hole was only large enough for an open palm to be placed inside. When his fist was holding the banana, the monkey could not remove his hand.

When the village returned to check his banana—coconut trap, the monkey would frantically try to pull out his fist with the banana. The creature was trapped. All the monkey had to do to escape was open his fist, let go of the banana, pull his hand out and run.

That's how monkeys came to be captured. They won't let go of what keeps them trapped, stuck, frozen in place.

And, that's exactly how humans get captured by life. The path to freedom is: let go of the banana.

Let go of bad habits that keep appearing over and over again;
Let go of fear based on bad experiences;
Let go of beliefs which no longer serve you;
Let go of needing others to like, accept and understand you;
Let go of perfection and other impossible standards;

Let go of thinking that you don't deserve happiness.
Let go of a relationship which is over, done, gone.

Branch out. Break out. Move on.

RETREAT

A DOZEN SIGNS YOU NEED A RETREAT

We are looking for happiness and running after it in such
a way that creates anger, fear and discrimination. So when
you attend a retreat, you have a chance to look at the deep
roots of this pollution of the collective energy that is
unwholesome.

—Thich Nhat Hanh

Be mindful about creeping burnout and boredom in your life. If you wait it out too long and delay taking action, you will find yourself exhausted and frustrated by all important things in your life—your relationships, your friendships, your work, even your leisure time. Here are signs you could benefit from a little time away and alone:

1. You need answers.
2. You feel bored, restless with your life.
3. You love yoga or meditation and want more.
4. You want to deepen your meditation practice.
5. You experience too much joyless striving.
6. You feel really stressed out, easily irritated.
7. Your mind is cluttered and confused.
8. Your life is in need of a new direction.
9. Your spiritual evolution has plateaued or declined.
10. You just need to get away, alone.
11. You're always rushing around.
12. You want to have more love, joy and peace in your life.

RIGID

BEING LESS RIGID

Nothing is softer or more flexible than water,
yet nothing can resist it.

—Lao Tzu

A Zen master asked one of his students to meet with him privately. He gave the student a mirror and instructed him to look into it.

"Is the face in the mirror exactly the same as the face on your body?" he asked.

"Yes" answered his student.

The Zen master requested him to look again into the mirror: "Is the face in the mirror exactly identical to the face on your body?" he asked.

"Yes" answered his student.

The Zen master slapped him very hard and asked: "Did the face in the mirror feel the pain which the face on your body felt?"

"No" answered the student.

Zen masters are well known for their unusual and sometimes harsh treatment of students in order for them to learn an important lesson. In the case of this student, the Zen master was trying to have him become less fixed in his views. It is likely his student was overly rigid. While it is an asset to have strong convictions and be self-confident, it is a liability to become authoritarian and arrogant. The problem with overly rigid people is that:

They see opinions and lifestyles other than theirs as wrong rather than different

They may publicly or privately reject people with whom they disagree

They can easily become intolerant, bigoted or self-righteous

They focus on absolutes rather than work to see possibilities.

However, if we can loosen our grip and be a little more elastic in our views, there are many benefits—a great deal of friction in life will be eliminated; we will experience much less stress; our ability to remain calm and deal skillfully with situations will improve; and, people will find us easier to get along with.

S

SADNESS

SAD OR GLAD? IT'S YOUR CHOICE

So much of our sadness or gladness depends upon the mind.
—Victor M. Parachin

An older woman in Hong Kong had two adult daughters. Though they were married and had families of their own, she constantly worried about them. Her first daughter was married to an umbrella salesman while the second was married to a noodle vendor.

On sunny days she worried, "No, not another sunny day. No one is going to buy any umbrellas and my daughter and son in law will have to close their shop down?" So, each bright, beautiful sunny day brought her anxiety.

When it was a rainy day, she worried, "No, not another day of rain. Noodles cannot be dried without the warmth of the sun. My daughter and son in law will be unable to sell noodles.

Thus, whether it was sunny or raining, the mother worried and worried, so much so that it began to affect not only her peace of mind but brought her pain of body.

As she walked by a Buddhist center, a monk standing outside noticed her look of despair and asked: "Why are you so sad?" After the woman explained her dilemma, the monk smiled and said: "The solution to your problem is very simple. On sunny days think of your younger daughter drying her noodles and the large volume she will sell. When it rains, think of the high sales that your older daughter's umbrella store will do."

Much of our sadness and gladness depends upon our mind. Train your mind to focus on the positive, the optimistic, the cheerful, the hopeful.

SAGE

ARE YOU A SAGE OR A FOOL?

Fools are asleep; sages are always awake.
—Mahavira

This should be a simple question with a simple "yes, I want to be a sage!" Yet, most people are fools and this includes many who follow a Buddhist path. Look at the reality and observe the difference between a sage and a fool.

Sages look within and use their minds to solve their problems. They understand that everything they need for dealing with life can be found within.

Fools seek help from outside. They pray to the Buddha and other deities asking for wealth, health, security, and relief from problems rather than strengthening their minds.

Sages cultivate the mind more than the body. While both are important, all things begin in the mind so they develop mind management to deal with life's poisons. Anger is replaced with patience; greed with generosity; ignorance or stupidity with wisdom.

Fools develop the body while completely neglecting the mind. Placing a total focus on a healthy body while the mind become weaker and sicker is counterproductive.

Sages develop spiritual friendships. They associate with people on a spiritual path providing mutual support, encouragement and accountability.

Fools have friendships but exclusively at levels which are superficial, frivolous, and one-dimensional. They have friends with whom they party, drink, use recreational drugs but no friends who offer spiritual insight and companionship.

SEEDS

A MONK ON A BOAT IN A LAKE

We have a seed of anger in us. We have a seed of compassion in us. The practice is to help the seed of compassion to grow and the seed of anger to shrink.
—Thich Nhat Hanh

With permission from the monastery Abbott, a monk borrowed an old boat and rowed out into the middle of a lake for his afternoon meditation session. It was a truly peaceful place to meditate as the boat gently floated.

After more than an hour of undisturbed silence, he felt the bump of another boat bang against his. With eyes still closed, he could feel anger swelling within himself at the careless boatman who didn't prevent the lake collision.

Upon opening his eyes, all he saw was an empty boat which he realized had obviously become untied from the dock and merely drifted out into the lake bumping up against his. Immediately, the monk experience a flash of enlightenment, one which would serve him well for the rest of his life. "The anger is within me," he thought to himself. "All anger needs is a bump from the outside to be triggered and provoked out of me."

From that moment on, whenever another person irritated him and he could feel even the slightest anger rising, he gently reminded himself: "The other person is an empty, floating boat. The anger is within me."

Life is all about response versus reaction. We have a choice between reacting with anger or responding with gentle awareness when an unpleasant situation arises.

SELF HEALING

SELF-HEALING THROUGH MEDITATION

Our minds possess the power of healing pain and creating joy.
If we use that power along with proper living, a positive attitude,
and meditation, we can heal not only our mental and emotional
afflictions, but even physical problems.

—Tulku Thondup

Tibetan Buddhist teacher and author Tulku Thondup feels strongly that meditation can generate healing—emotional, spiritual, mental and even physical. He believes this not only because it is a Buddhist teaching but also because he has witnessed the healing power of meditation.

One of his teachers had "mental" issues when he was a teenager revolving around serious anger management problems. He was so angry and destructive that his family had to tie him up to protect others and himself from his violence. Gradually, the young man embraced meditation placing his mind focus upon compassion. Through meditating upon compassion, he healed himself becoming an important scholar and teacher. As an adult, Thondup says his teacher is extremely "cheerful, peaceful and kind."

Another example Thondup cites is even more dramatic. A leading Tibetan lama had an attack of severe appendicitis while traveling in the remote countryside of Bhutan. A senior member of the country's government quickly arranged for a helicopter to take him to a hospital. Even though his pain was great, the lama, against the advice of doctors, declined surgery and healed himself via meditation combined with mantras.

Those anecdotes are inspiring reminders that our mind can and ought to be used to heal our various hurts, traumas, disappointments, injuries. No one has to live a damaged life. Meditation can be an invaluable tool for repair from human hurts.

SILENCE

THE WISDOM OF SILENCE

In spiritual life we cultivate sacred silence to regenerate
our inner being so that we can return to our daily
activities and to speech from a new perspective.
—Georg Feuerstein

Many find it difficult to meditate because it requires silence. Why is it hard to be silent? Here are some thoughts.

Speaking has become a very strong habit and strong habits, such as addictions, are hard to break. That may be why some people even speak to themselves when no one is around.

Silence is often used as a form of punishment in schools, in prisons, between couples and among friends so it comes with a negative social construct.

Talking makes us feel noticed and important whereas silence can makes us feel unnoticed and insignificant.

Silence means being alone with our thoughts, feelings and memories. Those are areas of our lives which are often suppressed and buried.

Just because something is difficult does not mean it should be avoided. In fact, very often our greatest gains and insight come precisely we take on a challenge. "Silence is golden" is a popular wisdom statement. Keep in mind that Buddhism highly recommends regular times of silence in our living via sitting meditation or a walking meditation in an outdoor nature setting.

The fact is that silence heals, creates wholeness and bring greater peace of mind and body. Studies consistently demonstrate that even a few minutes of silence lowers blood pressure, reduces the risk of hearts attack, boost immunity, decreases stress and more.

Conduct your own experiment with silence by bringing the wisdom of silence into your life, in your way. You could, for example, commit to silence over a meal whenever you are dining out. After all, you've likely ordered an expensive dish at the restaurant so why not enjoy it by eating mindfully and silently. If you are with someone ask him or her to join you in the silent meal. People don't talk during a concert preferring to pay attention to and enjoy the music. So, why engage in idle talk when eating out?

SIMPLICITY

SIMPLICITY IS SANITY

I advocate this maxim: 'Simplicity is sanity.' Have just enough to live moderately. Keep in mind the words 'good enough', rather than 'more,' 'better,' and 'best.' It's foolish to use the human mind only to think about wanting.
— Ajahn Sumano

When Ben Franklin was just beginning his career as a newspaper publisher, he wanted to do his work with integrity and honesty. As a result, he made the decision not to publish news or other information which he knew to be misleading, inaccurate or false. Even though material submitted to him for publication often came with sizeable financial incentives, Franklin wrote in his autobiography that he consistently refused to "print such things as might do real injury to any person."

Franklin's commitment to integrity was put to the test when a customer offered to pay Franklin a substantial amount to publish an article which Franklin knew was false and defamatory. In order to determine whether or not he should take the customer's money Franklin began the thought process to establish how much money he really needed to be comfortable coming up with this plan. He went home after work, bought an inexpensive loaf of bread, pumped a cup of water from his well. That was his supper—water and bread.

Upon retiring for the evening, he didn't go to his bed but instead wrapped himself in his large winter coat, lay down on the floor and slept until the sun rose. Then, he enjoyed a breakfast of water and last night's left-over bread. In his autobiography he said this experiment in simplicity came with "no inconvenience whatever" and added: "Finding I can live in this manner, I formed a determination never to prostitute my press to the purposes of corruption and abuse for the sake of gaining a more comfortable subsistence."

Simplicity is not only sanity but is the most powerful buffer against greed, excess, materialism, selfishness and attachment.

SLEEP

MINDFUL SLEEP

*In order to be able to sleep, we have to be able
to relax and let go of the day's stress and tension.
We can't make ourselves sleep; we can only allow
sleep to occur.*

—John Cline

Research indicates that up to 100 million Americans have sleep disorder. Added to that are the millions more who, while managing to sleep 7 hours a night, say they still wake up tired and drag through their days.

Insufficient sleep or poor quality sleep is considered a public health issue. People experiencing sleep disorder are also more likely to suffer from chronic diseases such as hypertension, diabetes, depression, and obesity, as well as from cancer, increased mortality, and reduced quality of life and productivity

While sleep issues are complex and sometimes evade a simple fix, there is a mindfulness technique which many have found to be very useful. It's a combination of conscious release breathing while focusing on ten points of the body—the two heels, the two buttocks, two shoulder blades, two elbows and two points on the back of the head. Conscious breathing releases tension in the body.

Here's how it's done:

While lying down bring your attention to the two eels. Take a deep inhale and then on a longer exhale instruct them "release and relax. Move up toward the two buttocks. Take a deep inhale and then on a longer exhale, instruct them to release and relax. Follow the same pattern for the two elbows and the two points on the back of the head. Cycle through until you drift off.

T

TASTE

TASTE TEST

There are some people who eat an orange
but don't really eat it. They eat their sorrow,
fear, anger, past, and future. They are not
really present, with body and mind united.

        —Thich Nhat Hanh

  A Zen teacher tells of visiting an incarcerated man. As a visitor he was carefully searched and not permitted to bring anything in for the prisoners. In the visiting area there was a small vending machine. There visitors were permitted to purchase items. So, the Zen teacher bought two chocolate bars, both for the man he was visiting.

  The visitor was immediately impressed by the way the prisoner dealt with the chocolate bars. First, their conversation stopped. He was very quiet as he carefully looked at the chocolate bar. After a few seconds and remaining very quiet, he carefully unwrapped the chocolate. Again, after looking at it for a few seconds he broke off a small piece, smelled the chocolate and then put it into his mouth. As it melted into his mouth, he closed his eyes as if to shut completely shut out all other stimuli. He then broke another small piece and another and another relishing every single part of the chocolate bar. He set the second one aside for another time.

  When was the last time you tasted something deeply and intentionally. For too many of us foods are taken for granted. We gobble and wolf things down. We eat while driving in a car. We seldom pause to savor the flavor.

Why not try this: at least once a week give your full attention to something you are consuming. For example, before you take that first sip of tea, look at it. Notice it's color. Observe the steam emerging. Feel the warmth of the tea container. Lift the cup and smell the aroma. Take a small, slow sip allowing your tongue to feel the warmth and experience the flavor.

TESTS

PASSING LIFE'S TESTS

Life tests and retests our emotional maturity. Whether we
meet those tests or fail is entirely up to us.
—Sivaya Subramuniyaswami

A woman in her early thirties saw her physician who, after conducting various tests, told her she had a life-threatening illness. He said it was "advanced," that she would become quite sick and that life expectancy with that condition was limited.

Of course, the information was frightening and devastating. She began slipping into self-pity, depression and anger. This was definitely a life test of her character. But, before long, she opted to take a different approach and asked herself a question which completely transformed her: "If the Dalai Lama were in my shoes, how would he feel? How would he handle this situation?"

Asking that question moved her to think differently about her life and issue. She concluded that the Dalai Lama would be accepting and would continue to act and live kindly. So she adopted as her life focus "just be kind." Anticipating she would be hospitalized off and on, the woman decided that she would be kind to everyone who entered her room—doctors, therapists, nurses, technicians, custodians, family, friends and other patients.

Once this was planted firmly in her mind, she experienced peace of mind in spite of the presence of a life threatening illness. It was extremely helpful for her to know that even while she was sick, her life could and would be of benefit to others.

Ironically, after more tests were done, it was discovered that the initial testing produced a "false positive", that she did not have a life threatening disease. While she was greatly relieved at the new assessment, she also realized that working with her mind about being ill was a significant learning moment. She resolved that she would continue being kind to everyone she met.

That woman's approach is one which anyone dealing with a problem or crisis can utilize.

When feeling discouraged and despairing, try asking yourself the question she did—"if the Dalai Lama were in my shoes, how would he feel? How would he handle this situation?"

You can insert the name of any person who inspires you. For example:

"If Mother Teresa were in my shoes, how would she feel? How would she handle this situation?"

"If Martin Luther King, Jr., were in my shoes, how would he feel? How would he handle this situation?"

"If Thich Nhat Hanh were in my shoes, how would he feel? How would he handle this situation?"

THANKS

THE BUDDHIST WAY TO 'GIVE THANKS'

Give thanks for everything in your world that cooperates to give you life and strength.

—Ignatius Loyola

Buddhism offers a mindful way of eating: it should be done with awareness and gratitude. Awareness that in consuming a meal we are beneficiaries of the planet: it's soil, it's water, the sun which nourishes growth, women and men who plant, cultivate, harvest, and make food readily available. Every meal is a gift given by the planet and by hard working individuals.

This awareness should result in gratitude along with a vow to be worthy of the gift and work to be of benefit to the planet and all on it. We should receive food with joy, with gratitude and with reverence. That's some of the energy contained within the following Buddhist ways of "giving thanks" for a meal:

From The Southeast Asian tradition:
Wisely reflecting I use this food not for mere pleasure, not for fattening, not for beautification, but for the maintenance and nourishment of this body, for keeping it healthy, for helping with the Spiritual Life; Thinking thus, I will allay hunger without overeating, so that I may continue to live blamelessly and at ease.

From The Zen Tradition:
First, let us reflect on our own work and the effort of those who brought us this food.

Second, let us be aware of the quality of our deeds as we receive this meal.

Third, what is most essential is the practice of mindfulness, which helps us to transcend greed, anger and delusion.

Fourth, we appreciate this food which sustains the good health of our body and mind.

Fifth, in order to continue our practice for all beings we accept this offering.

THREE

THREE SIMPLE MEDITATIONS

*Meditation training is not just for those chasing enlightenment
but also for those who are chasing a happier, more meaningful life.*
—Ajahn Brahm

Find a place where you can sit comfortably and quietly for a few minutes. Then, try one of these user friendly meditations to manage stress, anxiety and fear.

1. 50 Breaths, counting:

As you inhale, say "50" to yourself. On the exhale, say "49." On the next inhale, say "48" and on the next inhale, say "47." Follow this pattern always inhaling on the even number and exhaling on the odd number. When you get to zero, stop and rest in the stillness. You can repeat the exercise as many times as you need.

2. CPR meditation:

As you inhale, say to yourself "I am" and when you exhale say "calm." On the next inhale, say "I am" and when you exhale say "peaceful." On the third inhale, say "I am" and when you exhale, say "relaxed." Now you've done the CPR meditation (calm, peaceful, relaxed). Repeat as often as you need.

3. Peace, Love, Joy meditation:

As you inhale, say to yourself "Breathing in Peace" and as you exhale say "Breathing out Peace."

As you inhale, say to yourself "Breathing in Love" and as you exhale say "Breathing out Love."

As you inhale, say to yourself "Breathing in Joy: and as you exhale say "Breathing out Joy."

Repeat as often as you need.

THOUGHTS

ARE YOU A DOG OR A LION IN MEDITATION?

The affairs of the world will go on forever. Do not delay the practice of meditation.
—Milarepa

The Tibetan Buddhist teacher Milarepa (1052–1135) taught there are two ways to meditate—like a dog or like a lion. The analogy he used was that of a stick. When you throw a stick at a dog, he will chase after the stick. But, if you throw a stick at lion, the lion will chase after you. You can

113

throw many sticks in the direction of a dog but only once at a lion.

Here's how Milarepa taught this: "When you run after your thoughts, you are like a dog chasing a stick: every time a stick is thrown, you run after it. Instead, be like a lion who, rather than chasing after the stick, turns to face the thrower. One only throws a stick at a lion once."

Those who meditate like a dog experience thoughts as sticks being tossed at them by the mind. So, they constantly chase after the thought, follow the stick. It's endless. Those who meditate like the lion don't chase the stick or thought. They look for source of the thought, the mind which throws the stick. Like the lion they look carefully, come closely and discover that the "stick thrower", the mind flees under closer observation. Rather than try to shut out thoughts or make the mind blank, both of which are nearly impossible to do, turn and study the thought asking: *Where did you come from? Why are you interrupting me? You're annoying?* Then return to quiet, peaceful state of your natural mind.

This way you can meditate more like a lion than a dog.

TOILETS

CLEANING TOILETS MINDFULLY

Every friend, colleague and family member that I've ever known seems to find emotionally challenging. What's wrong with us? Life is so remarkable. By historical standards almost everyone in developed countries lives privileged lives full of riches.
—Ronald D. Siegel

People express surprise when Vietnamese Zen Master Thich Nhat Hanh says he enjoys cleaning toilets and does so mindfully, meditatively.

His mindful toilet cleaning practice begins with this realization—the simple joy of having a toilet! Growing up in rural Vietnam, no one in his village had a toilet of any kind. Even when he lived in a temple monastery which housed more than 100 people there was not a single toilet. "Around the temple there were bushes and hills, so we just went up on the hill," he explains.

In addition, there were no rolls of toilet paper on the hill and around the bushes. "You had to take dry banana leaves or hope to find some dead leaves you could use." Furthermore, he cites the fact that the population of Vietnam was twenty-five million people, the majority of whom did not have a toilet. Only the most wealthy had the luxury of indoor bathrooms.

So, the Zen master says that having a toilet to clean makes him very, very happy and he cleans it with joy and gratitude.

When we take our cultural comforts for granted, we deprive ourselves of joy. However, when we recognized how fortunate we are, especially when compared to many others on the planet, our scale of happiness rises.

TRANSFORMING

TRANSFORMING DIFFICULTIES

Difficulties will come no matter what we do. A spiritual practitioner can make use of those difficulties. You can turn any kind of mental, physical, financial or emotional difficulty into a benefit.
—Nawang Gehlek

No one is immune from difficulty, trouble, problems, sufferings. It is odd that so many people are surprised when a disappointment strikes. Buddhism reminds us that in life there is suffering. However, it also teaches that life's challenges can be transformed.

Consider the story of zen master Shichiri Kojun (1836–1900) who was meditating one evening when a thief with a sword broke into his residence. The burglar threatened Shichiri with his sword as he demanded money. Remaining in his meditation posture and seemingly barely affected by the thief, Shichiri said: "Do not disturb me. My money is in that drawer." Shichiri resumed his meditation. The intruder grabbed the money and, as he was preparing to make his exit, Shichiri said "you should thank a person when you receive a gift." Amazingly, the thief thanked him and left.

A few days later, the man was caught and confessed to stealing not only from Shichiri but from other homes in the neighborhood. Shichiri was subpoenaed and ordered to appear as a witness in court. When he was questioned by authorities, Shichiri surprised them by saying: "This man is no thief, at least as far as I am concerned. I gave him my money and he thanked me for it"

Because there were other witnesses who testified that the man was indeed the neighborhood burglar, he was convicted and sent to prison. However, when his sentence ended and he was released, the man returned to Shichiri becoming his disciple.

That story is well known in Japan and well loved among Japanese Buddhists. It is usually titled "The Thief Who Became A Disciple." It's inspiring because it reveals what happens when life opportunities are not wasted, dismissed, and marginalized. Shichiri had the ability to deal skillfully and compassionately with an unpleasant and uncomfortable situation, that of being robbed in his own home. By responding as he did, Shilchiri's actions impacted the thief in positive ways.

Life experiences should never be wasted. They should be transformed into benefit.

TREASURE

SEVEN TREASURES TO CULTIVATE

It is our duty to find the time and space, no matter how cramped and difficult our circumstances may be, to outgrow our immaturity and grow into our inherent loveliness. In this way we incline our life toward wisdom and compassion.
—Ajahn Sumano

One teaching of the Buddha is summarized in what is called the "Dhana" or Treasure Teaching. It provides a list of seven treasures which are to be cultivated in order to become a wise and noble human. This is the treasure teaching:

1. *The treasure of motivation.* Motivation is that unique combination of curiosity, joy and interest which compels us to bring good things into our lives and the lives of others.
2. *The treasure of right conduct.* Here we seek to live in ways that are harmless, ways which lead to peace and harmony. This involves not causing harm to ourselves or to others. It is the non-violence of body, mind, spirit and speech.
3. *The treasure of generosity.* Buddhist generosity involves not only an open wallet but cultivating an open heart, open mind and open spirit to be of benefit to others.

4. *The treasure of study.* We make time to read texts, hear teaching, attend retreats in order to deepen the mind and mature the spirit.

5. *The treasure of self respect.* We do not harbor negative views about ourselves nor do we disrespect our life recognizing we are Buddhas in progress.

6. *The treasure of respect for others.* All beings are to be treated with kindness and compassion, this includes our animal and insect neighbors on the planet. The treasure of respect for others is a call to celebrate the planets diverse beings.

7. *The treasure of wisdom.* It's not enough to merely have a great education and read many books. What's important is that information penetrates the heart and becomes wisdom.

Review the list and identify ones which need further development in your life.

TREES

TREES AS SPIRITUAL TEACHERS

Trees are the real givers as they are the most spiritually-advanced beings on earth.

—Swami Chaitanya Keerti

It's a well known fact that the Buddha attained his awakening or enlightenment while meditating under a tree. For that reason, his early communities met for meditation and instruction in forests under or near trees. The spiritual history of the East is tightly connected to trees. Most early ashrams—centers of meditation and learning—were carefully located in forest settings beyond the reach of urban life. Through the centuries of human spiritual evolution, forest areas and trees have been identified as best supportive for meditation, spiritual growth and evolution. Swami Keerti wisely observes that "trees are the real givers as they are the most spiritually-advanced beings on earth." Consider these ways that trees are spiritual teachers:

Their compassion is without discrimination or distinction. They provide shade and shelter in storms to all beings. Whether one is a sage or a criminal, safety of the tree is offered equally.

They practice acceptance and the contentment. Once a seed is planted, the tree grows where it has been placed.

Trees are referred to as the "lungs" of the earth. They produce the oxygen we breathe that oxygen is freely available to all.

Trees embrace life as it is. We humans wrestle with life, accepting some things but reject others. We are drawn to some people but turn away from others. A tree will grow in good soil, in rocky soil, in areas with ample water as well as where water is less available. It does its best regardless of the environment in which it finds itself.

They exhibit patience. Trees can live for centuries, much longer than human beings. Being in the presence of a tree is to learn the power of patience and to be reminded that life does not need to be frenzied and rushed.

Their roots go deep into the earth. This gives them the strength to withstand fierce storms of life.

Whenever you see a tree whether in a yard, along a road, as part of a forest, appreciate and absorb it's wisdom.

CARING FOR TREES

One should not destroy the trees.
Trees are homes and mansions.
> —Rig Veda

There are times when trees and plants—also "beings" with whom we share the planet—need a little human help. Do your part.

When a vicious typhoon struck Taiwan, the abbot of a Buddhist monastery surveyed the damage he saw that a Bodhi tree had been split in two by the fierce storm. Rather than further destroy the tree and turn it into firewood, the monk cared for it with all my heart." He lifted it, tied it together with ropes, and provided it support using sturdy bamboo props. "Now it has flourished into a tall, shady tree," he says.

On another occasion, another tree on the grounds collapsed onto its side, the result of heavy rains dislodging its roots. "It was no more than a rootless trunk and branches strewn across the ground," he recalls. Lifting it carefully, the monk planted it back into the soil and then watered it whenever the ground was dry. "As if by miracle, it not only took root and sprouted but has also matured into its present luxuriant form," he says proudly.

It's important to bring mindfulness not only into our personal lives but into the life around us as well.

U

UNEMPLOYMENT

RESTORING THE MIND WHEN JOB SEARCHING

It's a recession when your neighbor loses his job;
it's a depression when you lose your own.
—Harry S. Truman

Becoming unemployed almost immediately erodes mindfulness. That's understandable because unemployment and the task of job hunting create worries about paying the rent or the mortgage next month, about how quickly you can find a job, about whether or not you will find one with a comparable salary, etc.

Thus, it is vital to maintain focus and be highly mindful when job hunting. Here are four ways to bring mindfulness to bear when unemployed.

1. Bend. Cultivate flexibility. "Notice that the stiffest tree is the most easily cracked while the bamboo or willow survives by bending with the wind," observed Bruce Lee. Don't be rigid about what you can do and not do. Now that you're out of work be flexible about new horizons and opportunities. Listen to everyone who has an idea or suggestion.

2. Bask. A dictionary definition of bask is "to revel in and make the most of something." Enjoy the journey. Don't allow yourself to see only the negative. Unemployment is an ideal opportunity to regroup,

refocus and rethink. Much good can come from this period of time.

3. Breath. When discouragement infects you pause and take some intentional deep breaths as you inhale and exhale. As you breathe that way, repeat this affirmation: *I am capable. I am confident.*

4. Believe in yourself. There is no doubt that being unemployed plays havoc with one's self-esteem and self-confidence. However, sooner or later most people have this unwelcome issue in their lives. And, most of them weather it, land on their feet, with many saying "it was the best thing that ever happened to me!"

Beware of your mind. The mind has a mind of its own. When unemployed it can speak to you saying you're not good enough, smart enough, experienced enough, educated enough to get a great new job. That mentality can destroy all motivation when researching, applying and interviewing. Be aware when the mind is playing mind games with you. Stop it. Don't give in to it.

UNHAPPINESS

BEING AUTHENTIC AND NATURAL

For human beings it's best to be without chains.
—Kosho Uchiyama

Too many people are unhappy and the source of their unhappiness is that they aren't living the lives they really want to live. Too many people do what's been expected of them. They succumb to pressure from family, friends, society and culture.

Yet, freedom and its companion, happiness, is found when we live authentic and natural lives. The key for doing that is a very, very pure motivation, reason for doing what we do. That's the lesson in this story about a famous Tibetan hermit mediator named Geshe Ben. He was well into a lengthy retreat when he learned that those financing his retreat were coming to visit.

Immediately he began to clean up his cottage sweeping, dusting, wiping, and polishing his small shrine. Then he sat down in meditation position waiting for his sponsors to arrive. Abruptly, he began to realize

"What am I doing? This is all to simply make a good impression and it's fake. It's not me. It's now how I am."

Quickly jumped up grabbed a handful of ash from the stove by his side and flung it all over the shrine and the offerings. Later, a great Tibetan master called Padampa Sangye who heard about this described the incident as "the greatest offering in the whole of Tibet."

Be real. Be yourself. Be authentic. Then freedom and happiness will follow.

UNITY

BEING AT ONE

As human beings, we are all the same; each one of us
aspires to happiness and each one of us does not wish to suffer.
—Dalai Lama 14th

This may be the most common Buddhist joke around: What did the Buddhist monk say to the hot dog vendor? Answer: Make me one with everything!

Though this humor is well known, behind it is a powerful truth and that is unity or sameness or oneness. The problem in our lives and in our world is the opposite view: separation often called "duality" in Eastern philosophy. And, the issue with "duality" is that there is a split and that's not good. The very word "split" is used negatively in our own culture subtly acknowledging that unity and oneness are better. Some examples of the word "split" in our culture include:

"Splitting" the atom and creating a powerful, destructive nuclear explosion.

"You're splitting hairs" is spoken when an argument is spiraling out of control.

Couples "split" up usually creating more suffering for themselves, their children, their families and even their friends.

He has a "split" personality implying the person cannot be trusted emotionally.

"I have a "splitting" headache suggesting the violent act of being ripped in two.

There is a serious "split" in negotiations.

The Buddha frequently addressed the issue of personal duality and the problems it creates in our lives and for the planet. Duality occurs when an ego self emerges seeing itself a separate from others, better than others, smarter than others, more wealthy than others, more attractive than others, smarter than others. This creates competitiveness, jealously, envy, resentment and whole host of unhealthy emotions because is me versus you, us versus them, mine versus yours.

Duality "splits" people. Unity links people.

Moment by moment and day by day, let's consider the ways we tend to separate or split ourselves from others. Then, take remedial steps toward unity, making ourselves one with everything and everyone.

UNIVERSE

THE UNIVERSE HAS YOUR BACK

Remember that sometimes not getting what you want
is a wonderful stroke of luck.
—Dalai Lama 14th

During the Great Depression, a man who was completely uneducated, who could neither read nor write, learned of a job opening as a public school janitor in New York City. He applied but was turned down due to his illiteracy. Naturally he was disappointed and upset.

However, a friend helped him get a position selling cigars on the street. The man became a highly successful cigar salesman and deposited his commissions in the bank with the aid of a friend who wrote out the application form and deposit slips. After two or three years, he had a savings account of $30,000, at the height of the depression. He decided to withdraw some of his money. The bank teller instructed him to "write out a withdrawal slip for the amount you want." The said: "I can't read or write." Astonished, the teller said: "This is amazing! You've earned and saved thirty thousand dollars without an education! Where would you have been if you had been able to read and write?"

The man responded: "I would have been a janitor in Public School No. 17!"

When the Dalai Lama says, "Remember that sometimes not getting what you want is a wonderful stroke of luck," he means that we need to trust the Universe, remaining confident and calm even when events don't appear to favor us. We need to let the Universe have right of way.

UNWIND

UNWINDING THROUGH BATHING

I think a lot of contemplation happens in bathtubs.
It does for me. Nothing like a hot bath to ease the
tension and think about what's going to happen next.
—Sarah McLachlan

The next time you're in the shower rushing to get clean so you can move on to the next 'thing' consider this thought: what if you were more mindful about this daily action? Is it possible that something as routine as daily cleaning of the body could become a source of unwinding from stress and strain? Could the bringing of awareness to this seemingly mundane and routine ritual change the _act_ of bathing into the _art_ of bathing?

In her fine little book *Renew Your Life Through Yoga*, Indra Devi offers this alternative way of viewing the daily ritual of cleaning our bodies:

"Although many of us regard a bath as merely a method for getting clean—no more useful that the quick shower sandwiched in between getting up and getting dressed—the bath has been a ritual of relaxation for thousands of years. The Greeks and the Romans and the Turks all luxuriated in baths that were frankly Sybaritic (a sensuous pleasure). The Russians had their *bania*, the Finns their *sauna*, and in various parts of the world there are mud baths, hot springs, baths, and mineral baths.

Among the most pleasant of all is the Japanese bath, where you are able to sit comfortably in a barrel-like wooden tub filled with water up to your neck, without having to chill the upper part of the body or else lie semi-prone in a most uncomfortable position. I have often wished some enterprising person would introduce the Japanese tub into the American bathroom."

Even though you may not have in your home a Japanese wooden tub filled with water up to the neck, it's still possible to take this daily ritual of bathing and turn it into a moment of relaxation and renewal. The key for that to happen is mindfulness. Be fully present and truly enjoying those few moments. Then, the _act_ of bathing will become the _art_ of bathing.

USEFUL

WHY BENJAMIN FRANKLIN QUIT WORKING

The first stride in reaching for the things you want out of life is this: decide what it is that you truly want, then throw out all that is unnecessary.

—Christopher Hansard

At the age of 42 Benjamin Franklin quit working for living. He was done with it. Daily work in order simply to make money lost its appeal. By 1748, he had already developed a highly successful "media conglomerate" in his day. He owned a printing press, a publishing house, newspaper, a highly popular almanac series and was a postmaster, a position which ensured that his newspaper had a reliable delivery system.

Though he was making very good money from those enterprises and had the potential to make much more in the future, he was done accumulating money. He realized this was no longer a goal for him. So he quit, explaining to his mother, "I would rather have it said, 'He lived usefully than he died rich.'" So he sold off his enterprise.

This was a courageous move on his part and one which revealed his commitment to "serve others" as he told friends. Though he ceased working for money, he did not retire nor become a wealthy person of leisure. Instead, he began devoting himself to reading, studying, and experimenting. One of his experiments involved a way of making a home fireplace a more efficient source of heating. After several months he created what he called "Pennsylvania Fireplaces" similar to today's wood stove fireplace inserts. His invention became very popular and one of the first to purchase one was the governor of Pennsylvania who was so pleased with the effect that he endorsed and promoted Franklin's invention. He recommended that Franklin obtain a patent for his fireplace but Franklin declined and said in his autobiography: "As we enjoy great advantages from the invention of others, we should be glad of an opportunity to serve others with any invention of ours and this we should do freely and generously."

Unlike so many people, Franklin became clear about what he wanted out of life and how he wanted to live his life. The mere accumulation of wealth and the material things it brings simply wasn't enough. It never is.

V

VEGETARIAN

EAT LIKE THE BUDDHA

When I think of the suffering that meat eating brings,
I cannot bear the pain and anguish I feel within my heart.
—Nyala Pema Dundul

Vegetarianism was the diet of the Buddha and the majority of serious Buddhists worldwide follow that diet. Eating flesh food violates the first precept of Buddhism—to abstain from the taking of life. In order to justify a non-vegetarian diet, some individuals point to Tibetan Buddhism saying that they eat meat because it's hard to grow crops and vegetables in the high Himalayas.

While some Tibetans to eat meat, the preferred diet is vegetarian and, not surprisingly, meat eating has been questioned by Tibetan masters across the centuries. Many Tibetan Buddhist communities and lineages were completely vegetarian.

The highly respected teacher, Patrul Rinpoche, said that humans had turned animals into slaves forcing animals to "experience inconceivable torments." In *The Words of My Perfect Teacher*, he bluntly outlined the issue saying that animals domesticated by humans are "exploited until they die." He cited cattle, yaks, horses and sheep as an example noting: "They are milked, loaded down, castrated, pierced through the nose and yoked to the plow. Not one of them escapes this continual round of slavery. Horses and yaks continue to be loaded and ridden even when their backs are nothing but one big sore. When they can go no further, they are whipped and pelted with stones. The fact that they could be in distress or ill never seems to cross their owners' minds."

Similarly, Shardza Tashi Gyaltsen promoted vegetarianism teaching: "If someone is motivate by desire to eat the flesh of beings, then butchers will seize animals such as yaks or sheep and sever their minds from their bodies. How can those who consume meat and blood as food be followers of the Buddha? Such people pridefully consider themselves to be benefiting beings and protecting the weak, but their actions contradict the precepts. Meat eating is nothing but the cause of amassing terrifying evil."

VIRTUOUS

CHOOSING GOOD COMPANY

It is extremely important that we choose good company,
particularly if we are on a spiritual path, because our body,
speech and mind are very easily influenced by people withstand
whom we have close connection or frequent association.
—Dudjom Dorjee

We are constantly in the company of people—family, friends, colleagues, neighbors, people with whom we may serve on civic organizations, sporting events, and more. For this reason, Buddhism stresses the importance of having closest to us "good company". Another phrase used in Buddhism is "spiritual friends." People who are good company and spiritual friends are the ones whom we should have closest in our lives and in our hearts.

Why, because their influence upon us will be positive, encouraging, uplifting and a continuous source of motivation to continue moving forward. Spiritual friends bring energy to our souls.

Buddhism also recognizes that many who begin on the Buddhist path fall off because they lack good company and spiritual friends. In fact, their associations are the opposite. They have as their closest companions people whom Buddhism calls "unfortunate ones." These are individuals who exhibit little or no interest in spiritual growth and evolution. Meditating, attending retreats, reading Buddhist books and listening to teachings are not high priorities for them. Unfortunate ones cast a negative influence over our lives. Allowing unfortunate ones to become our closest inner circle of association obscures our motivation for growth, weakens our will, and erodes our confidence in the teachings we have received.

While will likely have a variety of friendships in our lives, it's important to apply Buddhist wisdom which reminds us to have, closest to us, "virtuous friends, noble friends, admirable friends", people in whose presence we continue to pursue enlightenment and seek ways to be of benefit to others9. These are the people in whose presence our time is well spent.

VISION

EQUAL VISION

Cultivation of virtues such as tolerance, adaptability, sympathy, mercy, equal vision, balance of mind, cosmic love, patience, perseverance, humility, generosity, nobility, self-restraint, control of anger, non-violence, truthfulness, moderation in eating, drinking and sleeping, simple living and endurance, is very necessary.
—Swami Sivananda

The quote above from Swami Sivananda is a comprehensive description of someone who is following a higher path in life. Of particular interest are the twin concepts of "equal vision" and "balance of mind" which Swami Sivananda includes. Both of those are very important in Buddhism as well as Hinduism.

Put simply, they mean we are to see the positive in a negative person, the good in an unkind individual, and Higher Self in the lower self of every being. Seeing the "saint in the sinner" is a common way of expressing the concept of equal vision and balance of mind. In Buddhist terms, equal vision means seeing Buddha nature in every being. Buddhism cautions against simply seeing beings in one dimension and from one perspective. When we don't practice equal vision and balance of mind, problems emerge as is revealed in this Eastern parable.

A devotee listened to his guru's teachings about equal vision and was highly impressed. It resonated with me deeply so he decided to practice it in his daily life viewing every human being and creature with equal vision. One day he was walking along a path when he suddenly saw an elephant running towards him. Though the man riding the elephant shouted at him to get out of the way because he was unable to control the elephant, the devotee decided to practice equal vision telling himself: "Like myself, this elephant has Buddha nature. I think kindly, warmly and compassionately about the creature approaching me." The elephant used its trunk to grab the devotee and toss him off the path.

Injured and upset the devotee returned to the guru explaining what had happened. "I practiced equal vision but received these injures because of it. You teaching of equal vision must be faulty," he said. The guru clarified offering this important insight. "In your eagerness to see Buddha nature in the elephant you ignored the warning of the elephant owner. I taught you that all beings have Buddha nature so why did you practice this recognition only in the elephant and ignore its owner? If you had respected him you would not have found yourself injured."

This story serves as a reminder how easily we treat beings differently. The devotee gave more weight, more creditably toward the elephant than he did to the owner. As you move through this day, be aware of ways in which you might view one person favorably but another unfavorably or one being more positively and another being negatively.

VOLATILE

A FINAL TEACHING OF THE BUDDHA

If you keep your practice steady, morning and night, summer and winter, there is nothing you cannot do and nothing that can harm you.

—Upaskashila Sutra

An account of the final weeks of the Buddha's life was carefully noted, remembered and later written down in the Pali Canon. Though aging and illness have taken their toll on his 8 decade old body, his mind is a lucid as always. Among the very last sentences he offered as a teaching to his closest disciples was this sentence: *Things fall apart; tread the path with care.*

Consider the two aspects of his teaching. First, "things fall apart." This is the reminder that life is unpredictable, uneven, erratic, and even volatile. One day a woman is well but the next day she receives a diagnosis of cancer; one day a man has a job but the next day he learns he is being laid off; one day life feels very good but the next day circumstances arise which leave a person feeling that his or her life is less than ideal. Almost no one would argue with the truth of the Buddha's observation "things fall apart."

The second half bring a sense of hope, stability, and balance to the first part of the teaching: "Tread the path with care." With those words the Buddha is reminding followers to be diligent, disciplined, attentive and tireless in adhering to the path. He is referring to his earliest lesson about the Noble eightfold path. To remain secure and stable in the changes and challenges of life, we must maintain a tight grip on the eightfold path—right view, right intention, right action, right speech, right livelihood, right effort, right mindfulness, right concentration.

We do not have to fall apart when "things fall apart."

That is the final teaching of the Buddha.

W

WEATHERING

WEATHING LIFE'S STORMS

A tree that is unbending, is easily broken.
—Lao Tzu

Julia Butterfly Hill came to be known and respected for her environmentalist stand when she lived in a 180 foot, 1500 year old California Redwood tree. Julia was committed to saving the tree from destruction by a logging company and was determined to remain as a 'resident' of the tree until she received assurances it would be spared. Her residency extended to 738 days during which time she affectionately name the tree "Luna."

After she'd been on the tree for two months, Julia heard a radio weather storm warning of seventy mile per hour winds coming her way. This terrified her and she was tempted to abandon "Luna" in order to find safe shelter. However, she knew that as soon as she left, the loggers would cut the tree down so she remained.

In her book, *The Legacy of Luna,* she describes herself as becoming physically tense and tight. Her teeth were clenched, her fists were clenched, her entire body was stiff and rigid. This was because she was convinced she would die during the violent storm. Julia knew that if she remained that way, she would snap. Then, as she observed other trees around her swaying in the wind, a life saving answer came to her. Like the trees, she began to release and relax into the storm. Like the trees around her which allowed themselves to bend and blow with the wind, Julia allowed her body to become softer and more flexible. She made it through the storm intact. And, she models precisely how all of us can make through the storms of life—by bending, flowing, arcing, and moving with the storm rather than against it.

WINDS

BEING STRONGER THAN THE EIGHT WINDS

A truly wise man will not be carried away by any of the eight winds: prosperity, decline, disgrace, honor, praise, censure, suffering and pleasure.
—Nichiren Daishonin

A popular Eastern wisdom story is often shared but the wrong lesson is applied. The story concerns a donkey, a father and his son. As they travel from their humble rural home toward a distant village, they both ride the donkey. When people see this, they criticize their cruelty for both sitting and over-loading the animal. Hearing the criticism, the father gets off and walks beside the donkey carrying his son.

Before long, people see this and criticize the son for "making" his elderly father walk while he, who is younger and stronger, sits comfortably on the animal's back. Hearing this criticism the father and son trade places. As they walk and people see this, they criticize the father for making his son do all the walking. Hearing this additional criticism, the father decides that neither of them will ride the donkey. Consequently, they both walk alongside the animal. Upon seeing this spectacle, people criticize the man calling him a "fool" for walking when he and his son could ride the animal.

Frustrated by all the criticism, the father throws the donkey off a bridge and they continue without an animal.

This story is told to demonstrate that people will always find reasons to judge and criticize us. Therefore we should ignore critics and their comments. That point is the minor theme of this parable. The major theme concerns the mind and developing one which is unfazed by criticism, unaffected by the opinions of others, unchanged by what people say and think about us.

That's why the 13th century Japanese Buddhist monk Nichiren Daishonin specifically taught that a "truly" wise person won't be carried away by any of the eight criticisms which come our way: *prosperity, decline, disgrace, honor, praise, censure, suffering and pleasure.* He is challenging people to develop strength of mind and character. It's not necessary nor is it useful to be overjoyed by praise and overcome with grief when criticized. Day by day, we need to work at becoming stronger internally and self-directed rather than being swayed by the various "winds" of life.

WORDS

THE POWER OF THOUGHTS AND WORDS

Thoughts are living things; they move; they possess form, shape, color, quality, substance, power and weight.
                                    —Swami Sivananda

How we think affects how we speak and how we act. It's quite simple. Positive thinkers speak and act positively. Negative thinkers speak and act negatively.

For that reason, we should never underestimate the power of our thoughts which become words and deeds.

Some time ago a teacher from Brazil wanted to demonstrate this power, to her students. She conducted an experiment using two glass jars of sealed rice. She arranged the class in a circle around the two jars of grains.

Then, she asked the students to say bad things to one of the cups—things people might hear in everyday life, like "you are useless," "you are stupid," "you're a loser" and "you can't accomplish anything." That jar was labeled "hate cup."

To the second glass, the teacher asked the kids to say things they would like to hear from everyone. The kids used such expressions as "you are special," "you can accomplish anything," "you're cool" and "you are smart." That jar was labeled "love cup."

A few days later, the rice in the "love cup" fermented naturally while the rice in the "hate cup" became dark and moldy.

When asked why she did the rice experiment with her class, the teacher said she wanted to impress upon her students the value and significance of focusing on the positive side of life more than the negative.

That experiment reinforces this truth: Positive thinking produces positive results. Negative thinking produces negative results. So be positive, even when you are going through hard time.

WORLD

MAKE THE WORLD A BETTER PLACE

Be the change that you wish to see in the world.
—Gandhi

You can change the world! And, you're not alone. There are people like you—kind, compassionate, concerned—all over this beautiful planet. Here are a dozen ways you can do your part to make the world a better place.

Practice right speech. Speak quietly, gently and don't gossip, ever. Avoid complaining.

Be polite. Never be rude to other beings. There's no need for that, period.

Smile—a lot. Smile at your family, friends, neighbors, colleagues and especially strangers.

Play by the rules. Don't seek exemptions or privileges for yourself.

Act properly. Live by your values, morals, ethics. Be an example to yourself, to others.

Consume consciously. Ask yourself, "do I really need it?"

Cultivate kindness. Be kind to all especially those who are unkind to you.

Live with purpose. Don't drift; don't live aimlessly.

Promote nonviolence. Avoid injuring or hurting any being. This includes animals, birds, insects.

Keep the planet clean. Don't litter; don't smoke, don't pollute.

Change your diet. Switch to vegetarian. This helps animals as well as environment.

Give. If you have a lot, give a lot. If you have a little, give a little. Generosity is a virtue.

Y

YES

SAYING 'YES' TO _ALL_ OF LIFE

Try saying yes to more things that are not your preference.
—Rick Hanson

Musician John Lennon says that he first began falling in love with Yoko Ono when he viewed an exhibition of her art at a gallery in London. One of her exhibits required a viewer to climb to the top of a shaky ladder in a dimly lit room. At the top of the ladder was a telescope. Peering through it, a visitor had to make out the faint, barely perceptible, letters of a single word. Though the word was small and simple it struck Lennon with a powerful insight and impact.

The word was "YES."

Yoko Ono's artistic display was a powerful art tool clearly demonstrating that getting to a "YES" in life means assuming some fear, some stress, some anxiety. Those who are willing to climb that shaky emotional ladder and look ahead are the women and men who enter bold, new chapters in their lives.

Those who are unwilling—and sadly that's the majority of people—remain frozen in place and space.

Are you in the group that is willing or unwilling.

Whatever life brings your way, always be willing to climb that shaky latter and say YES' to life.

YES, I can deal with this challenge.

YES, I can manage this pain.

YES, I will do whatever it takes to adjust and adapt.

YES, I need support and will turn to the right people for it.

YES, I will live in ways that move me forward.

YES, I will focus on the positive.

YES, I will maintain hope about my future.

YES, I will learn from disappointments, shortcomings, failures.

YES, I accept the twists and turns which life brings me.

YES, YES, YES to life!

YOKES

FREEDOM NOW

Free at last, free at last, thank God almighty we are free at last.
—Martin Luther King, Jr.

All of the Buddha's teachings are directed at freedom which could be understood as another word for enlightenment. One such freedom teaching is from the "Yoke Sutra." A yoke is commonly understood as a wooden cross beam placed over an animal's neck allowing it to pull a load such as a wagon or plow. Yoke, however, is also another word for slavery. In the Yoke Sutra, the Buddha reminds us that we are shackled by yokes of our own choosing. He identifies four "yokes" which keep us down and hold us back from experiencing the fullness and freedom we all long for in life. These are the four:

1. The yoke of sense experiences—our habitual pursuit of sense pleasures such as the latest electronic device, the newest car, the most exotic trip, etc.
2. The yoke of becoming—our dysfunctional way of creating an alternative reality by the thoughts we think and the stories we tell ourselves.
3. The yoke of views—being bound to our rigid perspectives causing us to become intolerant of other viewpoints and positions.
4. The yoke of ignorance—not paying attention to ourselves, our

experiences, and failing to understand what's really going on with us and in our lives.

The Buddha urges us to become aware of the ways we burden ourselves by these four "yokes" or attachments. In order to be free and experience enlightenment we need to shed four yokes or chains which hold us captive. The way to do that is via awareness and mindfulness.

Z

ZEN

TEN ZEN QUESTIONS

Asking leads to revealing. Questioning uncovers insights. From time to time ask yourself 'why' or 'why not'?

—Victor M. Parachin

Go over this list today and see what thoughts, impressions, conclusions arise.

1. When was the last time I did something for the first time?
2. Am I experiencing joy daily?
3. Am I bringing joy to others daily?
4. Who do I love and what am I doing about it?
5. What have I done recently which is memorable?
6. Does it really matter what others think of me?
7. Where will I be in three or four years if I keep heading in this direction?
8. Am I who I want to be?
9. Who are my spiritual friends and how much time do I spend with them?
10. How would I like others to remember me after I die?

Return to this list in six months reviewing it again. What's changed?

Readers Guide

1. What is the difference between wisdom and knowledge?

2. Why is anger so prevalent in society? Identify ways women and men could better manage and limit anger.

3. Buddhism stresses the importance of right association or right friendships. What are the qualities to look for in people to establish healthy relationships?

4. Describe acts of generosity which you have personally witnessed recently.

5. Rather define enlightenment, identify persons you consider to be enlightened and explain why you see them that way.

6. It's easy to remain balanced and calm when things are going well but why are so many of us so easily thrown off balance when challenges emerge? What tools and skills are needed for equanimity?

7. What does it mean that all beings have Buddha nature?

8. Why do people meditate? What benefits can come from meditation?

9. What is right effort and when is it vitally important?

10. Generally, most people try to be kind to those they know. However, how can kindness be expanded to include every person we come into contact with.

11. Sooner or later, loss and grief comes to everybody: a loved one dies, health is lost, a friendship fractures. What are skillful ways to grieve more mindfully.

12. When can guilt be good. Provide real life examples.

13. Identify simple ways which can strengthen happiness.

14. The concept of impermanence—the fact that everything changes—is foundational in Buddhism. Why do we become upset and unsettled when change appears? How can the concept of impermanence help?

15. Too many people feel confined, limited, trapped and even imprisoned by their lives. What steps could they take to self-liberate themselves.

16. Do you agree with the statement "a positive mind leads to a positive life?" Why or why not?

17. Practicing 'noble silence' is important in Buddhism. Why is silence golden and when are ideal times or moments to remain silent?

www.ingramcontent.com/pod-product-compliance
Lightning Source LLC
Chambersburg PA
CBHW011201090426
42742CB00020B/3413